AEROFILMS GUIDE

The
Thames Path

Helen Livingston

IAN ALLAN
Publishing

THE THAMES PATH

Based on an original idea by
Richard Cox of Aerofilms

Designers Michael D. Stride and
Robert C. Wilcockson
Series Editor Rebecca King

Published by Ian Allan Ltd, Shepperton, Surrey;
and printed at their works at Coomblands in
Runnymede, England

Contents

Main picture: Buscot Weir
Title page: Winter Hill, east of Marlow

Other titles in this series:

The South Downs Way

The Cotswold Way

The South Devon Coast Path

The Leeds-Liverpool Canal

**Offa's Dyke (South) and the
    River Wye Valley**

THE THAMES PATH

THIS, THE NEWEST National Trail, is some 213 miles (340km) long and unique in that follows a major river from beginning to end. The Thames rises inconspicuously in a field near Cirencester then makes its way past villages of Cotswold stone, meanders through open, level countryside and peaceful watermeadows, skirts famous and historic towns and cities and then flows through the wooded reaches of the Thames valley before finally entering the city of London and ending at the Thames Barrier.

Throughout this journey the Thames Path provides level, easy walking suitable for the whole family. There are no windy heights or isolated stretches to be tackled here, and the path can be joined at dozens of easily accessible points. This makes it ideal for short strolls, perhaps combined with a trip on the river or a visit to a place of interest, as well as for day-long hikes undertaken

Slow let us trace the matchless vale of Thames...
The Seasons, Thompson

by those wishing to cover longer sections. Accommodation, refreshment and public transport are also readily available at regular intervals.

Much of the path, of course, follows

the Thames towpath, a route which has been used for centuries as barges plied their way up and down the river. From time to time the path changes banks, and the bridges - upwards of a hundred - are a fascinating feature of the walk. So, too, are the locks and weirs which make the river navigable. Discoveries of all kinds are to be found along the Thames Path and the aim of this book is not only to get the walker safely from A to B, but to provide an insight into the history of this great river and into the lives of the people who have been influenced by it.

In this book the Thames Path is described in detail from its source as far as Richmond, at which point the river becomes tidal and the path follows both banks. This final section is described on page 174.

Top left: Kemble, the first village on the walk

Left: Looking eastwards over Hurley

Right: The Radcliffe Camera, Oxford

Below: Kew Gardens, at the end of the walk

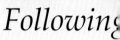

Following

The Thames Path is a new Countryside Commission National Trail and work involving the replacement of stiles and footbridges, signposting and the opening up

VERTICAL PHOTO-MAPS

The path is plotted on vertical photographs using a scale of 1:10,000 (0.6 miles:3.9ins, 1km:10cm).

GENERAL TEXT

Points of specific interest and information relevant to that particular stretch of the route accompanies every photo-map. It is always advisable to check opening times of places of interest in advance of a visit.

DIRECTION

In general, the right-hand edge of the photo-map joins the left-hand edge of the map on the next spread. However, to make the direction of the route absolutely clear, arrows indicate how the maps link together.

SYMBOLS

The following symbols appear on the photo-maps for information and to help the walker get his bearings.

Railway station

Place of interest

Pub or hotel

Car park

Church

River Thames

The route

Roads

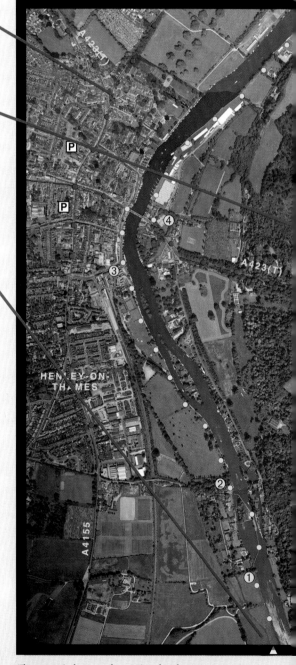

The vertical photography used in the photo-maps is taken from an average height above sea level. This means that the scale of the photography will alter slightly as the contours of the ground vary. The photo-maps are constructed by piecing together a series of photographs to make each page. They are intended to give a

the Route

…new linking sections is still being carried out. This book describes the exisiting route in detail, and gives detailed directions on how to negotiate the missing links.

Henley-on-Thames to Cookham

13 miles (20.75km)

Between Henley-on-Thames and Cookham the Thames Path passes through scenery in which everything seems to be on a larger scale than before. First, the long regatta course, then the tumbling weirs of Hambleden, the great meander bend and, beyond Marlow, the ascent up through Quarry Wood on to Winter Hill for a gloriously expansive view over the Thames valley before dropping back down again to reach Cookham.

MARSH LOCK is backed by a wooded hillside which adds an extra charm to the waters of the weir superbly viewed from the wooden causeway. There was a flashlock here in the 1500s and the poundlock was first constructed in 1773.

Henley is famous for its regatta which dates from 1839, a time when Henley was on the important coaching route from London to Oxford. Many distinguished guests stayed in the inns, including the Duke of Marlborough, who had his own room at the Red Lion. Travellers by coach would cross the splendid bridge which replaced an earlier timber structure that had been washed away by the river in March 1774. The 16th-century church stands near the bridge, its tall battlemented tower looking down on the scene. Charles Dickens described Henley as 'the Mecca of the rowing man', and it was the straight river reach between Henley and Temple Island that first attracted the rowing men to Henley. The races were first organised as a regatta in

1839 and the event became royal in 1851, under the patronage of Prince Albert. Today the regatta attracts rowing crews from all over the world who compete for the various cups and prizes.

ROUTE DIRECTIONS

1. Turn left along the towpath towards Marsh Lock. On reaching the lock bear right to follow the causeway to Marsh Lock Island and return to the river bank at Mill Lane along another long wooden causeway.
2. Turn right to continue along the towpath which joins a promenade as you approach Henley Bridge.
3. Where the promenade ends join the road and follow it past the Angel on the Bridge pub. Turn right to cross Henley Bridge.
4. Turn left on the other side of Henley Bridge and bear round to the left back on to the tow-path with the river on your left (NB during Regatta Week in early July the path is moved inland, a fact recognised in the dedication of the right of way).

Most famous of all Thames-side towns – Henley

SCALE FOR PHOTO-MAPS
The scale-bar represents a distance of 0.310 miles (0.5km).

SECTIONS OF THE PATH
The route from Thames Head to Richmond has been divided into sections that can be comfortably walked in a day. Each of these sections opens with an introduction and the distance involved is given.

COMPASS POINT
Every photo-map is accompanied by a compass point for ease of orientation.

ROUTE DIRECTIONS
These numbered route directions correspond to the numbers shown in yellow on the photo-maps.

OBLIQUE PHOTOGRAPHS
These photographs bring a new perspective to the landscape and its buildings. All the subjects chosen can either be seen from, lie on, or are within easy reach of the path.

…pictorial representation of the ground and strict accuracy of scale throughout cannot be guaranteed. There may also be a mismatch in areas of extreme relief – ie where the land is steepest. These problems have been kept to a minimum, in particular close to the main route of the walk.

THE THAMES RISES in the silence of a Cotswold meadow called Trewsbury Mead, some 3 miles (4.8km) south-west of Cirencester, under the shadow of an ancient hillfort. It is marked by a simple stone beside an ash tree. The source of any great river is a magical spot, and though the Thames is small compared to the giants of the world, flowing only some 215 miles (344km), Thames Head possesses a magical air. Yet the source of the Thames is something of an enigma, for not only is water rarely seen at the little ring of stones under the ash tree, but its claim to be the source has been disputed in favour of Seven Springs near Cheltenham. But Seven Springs is the source of the tributary stream, the Churn, which has always been regarded as a separate river. Perhaps this dispute arose because of the frequent lack of water at Thames Head. For much of the year the first 2 miles (3.2km) of the Thames is merely a winding, grassy hollow.

It is a tantalising beginning, a teaser, a start which sends us downstream in search of 'the first water'. Canal, road and rail surround the Thames Head spring. The tree-clad embankment of the derelict Thames and Severn Canal stands just a few yards off, while near by trains ply the busy line through Kemble. Legend holds that the Romans fought a battle here, and a couple of fields away runs Foss Way, the great frontier road constructed in the early years of the Roman occupation and in continuous use as a line of communication ever since. Just down-valley from Foss Way stands the Lyd Well, mentioned in Domesday, and thought by some to have been dug by the Romans. Today it is hidden behind a wall and sheltered by trees. Thames water can sometimes be seen here.

Thames Head to Cricklade

11 miles (17.5km)

This first section of the Thames Path follows the main headwater stream from the Thames Head spring, between lush meadows and stone-built villages on the lower slopes of the Cotswolds. It passes among the lakes of the Cotswold Water Park to Cricklade and the confluence of the Thames and Churn.

ROUTE DIRECTIONS

1. From the source, follow the footpath across the meadow and climb the stile in the fence. Carry on and go across the steps over the stone wall.

2. Follow the trackway across the next meadow, with the shallow, marshy valley on your left. Go through the gate and cross over the A433, the Foss Way.

3. Climb over the stile and go down the stone steps. Bear right across the field, with the dry bed of the Thames on your left (note the smashed remains of a small, stone footbridge).

4. Go through the gate in the top right-hand corner of the meadow, with the drystone walls around Lyd Well on your left.

5. Follow the track and then bear left over the field, crossing a footbridge over a tributary channel. Climb the stile to reach the A429 road at the first real bridge over the Thames.

6. Cross the A429. Follow the footpath signed to Ewen, keeping the young Thames on your right. Go through the waymarked gate and bear right alongside the Thames channel to the road at Parker's Bridge.

A429

KEMBLE

9

1. Turn left and follow the road towards Ewen. Take the first road on your right. Cross the Thames and immediately beyond the bridge (before you reach Home Farm), turn left over the stile. Follow the path, with the river on your left, and cross the stile into the belt of woodland, following the river round to the right.

2. Cross the stile and bear left, with two pylons on your right. Go under the electricity transmission lines and keep on round the field. Cross the stile, and continue with the Thames and a belt of woodland on your left.

3. Go over the next stile, then continue across another stile and along the path beside the mill race to Upper Mill Farm (the Thames itself follows the winding channel on your right, marked by the belt of bushes and willow trees).

THROUGHOUT THE YEAR there is water in the Thames near Ewen, though you may have to walk beyond the bridge near Home Farm to find it – a mysterious, wonderful beginning, where a tiny weir holds back the trickle as it sets forth for London and the sea.

There was formerly a chapel at Ewen, but during the last century it was moved stone by stone to nearby Kemble and rebuilt as the south transept of Kemble church.

At Ewen the Thames is undeniably becoming a river, for here on the right-hand side of the road, just beyond Parker's Bridge, is Mill Farm. This was the highest mill on the Thames, where there was just enough water to turn a mill wheel. Today we may wonder at the foolhardy miller who built a watermill where for eight months of the year the river is dry. But prior to the extensive gravel extraction just downstream, and before the construction of the Thames and Severn Canal in 1792, there was water in this

reach. There were five mills along the 7-mile (11.2km) stretch of the infant Thames from the source to Waterhay Bridge, and a further two, Washbourne and Pool Keynes, on tributary streams. Of the other four mills on the main stream, and thus on the Thames Path, there was Upper Mill, now Upper Mill Farm, which the Thames Path approaches along the old canalised mill

Upper Mill Farm

Kemble House and the village church

stream. Its mill wheel was demolished in the 19th century. Ashton Mill in Ashton Keynes is now a beautiful private house. Lower Mill, now on the edge of the Cotswold Water Park, was, until the early years of this century, still grinding grain to make cattle feed for local herds. Finally, Kemble Mill, which stands about half-way between Upper and Lower Mills, still retains its millstones.

Upper Mill Farm

① ② ③ ④ ⑤ ⑥ ⑦

SOMERFORD KEYNES

N

SOMERFORD KEYNES, like Ashton Keynes, the next village along the river, owes the second half of its name to the de Kaines family, local landowners who came from Cahagnes in Normandy with William the Conqueror. 'Somerford' means a place where the river could be forded in summer, probably the highest ford on the Thames. The ancient All Saints' Church at Somerford Keynes, which stands beside the manor house, has a Saxon porch way belonging to an earlier church and a carving from the early 11th century showing two dragons facing each other.

Farmland between Ewen and Somerford Keynes

ROUTE DIRECTIONS

1. Turn left at Upper Mill Farm and cross the footbridge over the former mill race. Go down the drive and over another stile to continue along the path by the wind pump.

2. Cross over another stile and footbridge and walk down the next field, with the hedge on your left. Turn left over the stile and bear right to cross a stile and footbridge beside a double gate.

3. Bear diagonally across the next field and through a squeeze-stile beside a cottage. Cross the next field to emerge at the edge of Somerford Keynes by a stone stile near the old school.

4. Turn right along the driveway towards the church and then left through a gate into the churchyard. Cross the churchyard and go through a wicket-gate, then walk down the field following the path signed to Oaksey Moor. Cross over the footbridge and go straight over the next field, heading for Kemble Mill.

5. At the mill cross the footbridge over the Thames and follow the path to the footbridge over the mill stream, by the cottage wall, and continue along the path to the lane.

6. Turn left along the lane, with Kemble Mill on your left, then turn left along a path which leads you round the lake in Neigh Bridge Country Park to Neigh Bridge. Bear right along the road and turn left at the crossroads, along the Water Park Spine Road.

7. Follow the road and cross over the Thames. Turn right along a track to Lower Mill Country Park. Continue past Lower Mill Farm, with flooded gravel pits on your left. At the double gates turn right to cross over a footbridge across the Thames. Keep straight on along the footpath, bearing left between flooded quarries and then the trees of Freeth's Wood.

Spine Road

ROUTE DIRECTIONS

1. Continue and cross the B4696. Carry on along the path, with the Thames on your left, and follow Church Walk into Ashton Keynes.

2. Turn left along High Road and then right along Back Street. Just beyond the right-hand turn in the road turn left on to the footpath, with Kent End Farm on your left. Turn right over a metal stile and continue along the edge of the field.

3. Cross another metal stile and bear left up a gravel drive to the road. Cross the road and turn right over a stone stile (signed footpath to Waterhay), into the gravel drive leading to a sports field.

4. Cross the sports field, with the pavilion on your right, and go over the stile. Go diagonally right across the field and pass through the gate, then cross the remains of a stone-arched bridge over a stream.

5. Follow the path alongside the meadow, with the stream on your left, and go through the gate. Bear to the right across this meadow and reach a gate on to the road.

The church at Ashton Keynes stands by the B4696 to the west of the village

THE THAMES, still no more than 10ft (3m) wide, flows alongside the High Road in Ashton Keynes and divides the stately old houses from the street. Because of this each house has its own little bridge, some 20 in all, beneath which the shallow river ripples over its gravelly bed.

At the end of Church Walk is Ashton Mill, the next of the former watermills along the Thames. Here, there are the bases of four medieval crosses where sermons were once preached, while the moated fields surrounding Church Farm to the west of the church are all that is left of a monastery – the first of many ecclesiastical remains to be found along the Thames. The farmhouse may have been part of the monks' living quarters.

Ashton Keynes was in earlier times of some importance, but by 1826 William Cobbett, the famous chronicler, was able to describe it as a spot with which 'I was very much stricken. It is now a straggling village; but, to a certainty, it has been a large market town, there is a market cross still standing in an open place in it; and there are such numerous lanes, crossing each other, and cutting the land up into such little bits, that it must, at one time, have been a large town. It is a very curious place...'

1. Go through the gate and turn left along the road, then left again across the car park for Waterhay Bridge (Cotswold Water Park). Go over a concrete bridge and turn left through the gate, bearing left on to a bridleway.

2. Turn right at the junction of tracks and follow the trackway, with a quicksand lake on your left, note the danger signs. Follow the track round to the left, with Manorbrook Lake, a game-fishing area, on your right.

3. Continue to follow the bridleway, bearing right back to the Thames. Carry on along the track beside the Thames, past Bournelake Bridge and then away from the river, to turn left and cross a footbridge over a stream.

4. Continue along the track and then turn right, heading back to the river at the foot of Hailstone Hill. Do not cross the river at the footbridge, but turn left to follow the river along a permissive path to the old railway bridge.

5. Go under the bridge and continue with the river on your right to the line of the former North Wiltshire Canal which crossed the Thames here by aqueduct.

BETWEEN SOMERFORD KEYNES and Bournelake Bridge the Thames and its tributary headwaters thread their way between gravel workings, most of which have filled naturally with water. This is the Cotswold Water Park, and it will eventually cover some 12,000 acres (4,860ha). It has completely altered the nature of the area, changing it from meadowland to one of the largest wetlands in Britain. The flora and fauna are adapting to suit the alterations. Already, several of the flooded quarries have been designated as nature reserves, while others are used for watersports. The Thames is throughout a lowland river, without a dramatic mountain course. Nowhere does it tumble from rock to rock in headlong, giddy descent. Its source is only about 360ft (109.4m) above sea level and there are no waterfalls along its length – though the foaming weirs introduce lines of white water – and it is content to meander through meadows and among woodlands, quietly enjoying its own flood plain. All the way down to the sea, with one small exception at Clifton Hampton, where sandstone crosses the river bed, the Thames flows over its own deposits rather than rock: sometimes gravel and sometimes fine-

grained alluvium. From the source downstream to its confluence with the River Thame, at Dorchester-on-Thames, the Thames is also known as the Isis. Above Oxford the river is more frequently referred to as the Isis, and many maps use only this alternative name.

During the Middle Ages it was thought that the name Thames was a combination of 'Thame' and 'Isis', the latter not descended from the Egyptian goddess but from the Celtic *Is*, meaning water. It is thought that this belief started when Julius Caesar referred to the Thames as Thames is. Thereafter, this view developed down through the years so that, during Elizabethan times, the Poet Laureate Michael Drayton used it and wrote of the marriage of the Thames and the Isis, with Isis as the bride and Thames the bridegroom.

Hailstone Hill

Cricklade to Lechlade

10 miles (16km)

In early times Cricklade was the head of navigation along the Thames, and even today the river from here to Lechlade is navigable by small craft. There is no towpath along this reach, and the walker follows footpaths and roads which at times are several fields' length from the river. Despite one nasty stretch of A road (which the Thames Path will one day avoid), this is a remote and tranquil section of the walk, bypassing most settlements. At Inglesham it rubs shoulders with the solemnity of the little 12th-century church and passes the ruined entrance of the Thames and Severn Canal, to join the Thames towpath at last.

EVERY CRICKLADE HOUSEHOLDER possesses grazing rights on North Meadow, the 114-acre (46ha) pasture by the Thames, that today is managed as a nature reserve. The grazing rights run from 12 August to 12 February, during which time there is free access, while for the remaining six months access is along specified footpaths only. This allows a crop of hay to to be grown organically, in the time-honoured way which produces a lush growth of rare meadow flowers, including snakes head fritillaries (the flower above all other associated with Thames meadows in the past), marsh marigold and water crowfoot as well as the more common buttercups and celandines. However, under the current plans, the official Thames Path will be diverted along the other bank of the Thames, away from North Meadow.

ROUTE DIRECTIONS

1. Cross the canal and go over the stile into North Meadow, now a nature reserve, and continue alongside the Thames till you are forced to turn left away from the river across a rough field.

2 Go over the footbridge and through the gap in the hedge and then follow the footpath as it bears to the right back to the river.

3. Cross the River Churn by the wooden footbridge then cross the field to go through a gate and over another footbridge. Go over the next field and up the slope to the road.

4. Turn right along the the road and cross the Thames by High Bridge at the bottom of Cricklade High Street. Continue up High Street, passing St Mary's Church on the old town wall, and then turn left into Abingdon Court Lane.

5. Turn left out of Abingdon Court Lane, then right on to a track and across rough land to a stone stile. Cross the stile and bear left. Cross the next stile beside a farm gate.

Cerney Wick, north-east of Cricklade by the Cotswold Water Park

6. Follow the path beside the Thames over a farm bridge and under the A419(T) bypass. In the third field beyond the bypass turn left to cross the Thames by Eysey footbridge.

CRICKLADE IS ANCIENT. A venerable small town of Cotswold stone, with a striking church tower, narrow streets and two medieval crosses, it stands just west of Roman Ermin Way, the great road from Newbury to Cirencester which crossed the Thames here, presumably by ford. There was a Roman villa near the High Street and a substantial village associated with the villa site but there is no evidence to suggest continuous occupation since Roman times, and it seems likely that the line of the Ermin Way river-crossing was lost soon after the Roman withdrawal. However, St Augustine and the Celtic bishops may have met here early in the 7th century. The present town owes much of its layout to the creation of a Saxon burgh, associated with a new river crossing and probably founded by King Alfred towards the end of the 9th century. It consisted of a square earthwork enclosure, which in later times was topped by stone town walls and formed part of the defence system of Wessex, built by King Alfred to ward off the Danes. The town is first mentioned in the Anglo-Saxon Chronicle for AD905: '...Athelwold led the host in East Anglia to begin hostilities with the result that they harried the whole of Mercia until they came to Cricklade and there they crossed the Thames...' and further entries explain how the Danes brought their ships up the river to Cricklade in

AD905 and again in 1016. A now wholly discounted legend has it that Cricklade should be rendered 'Greek-lade', having been a colony of Greek scholars long before Oxford grew to be a seat of learning. A successor to this college was said to have been founded here by Penda, King of Mercia. This institution, so goes the tale, was removed to Oxford by Alfred the Great. Indeed, University College, Oxford, used to claim that Alfred was in fact its founder. This is untrue, for the college was founded by William, Archdeacon of Durham, in 1249.

St Mary's Church, on the line of the northern town wall, may incorporate the remains of one of the town's gatehouses, or a chapel associated with the gatehouse. This little church, mainly Norman, is associated with the remains of a medieval priory to which it is said to be connected by an underground passage. A group of houses in the High Street are the slight remains of the priory founded in 1231 by the Knights Hospitallers. St Sampson's, one of the great wool churches of the Cotswolds, has a magnificent Tudor tower.

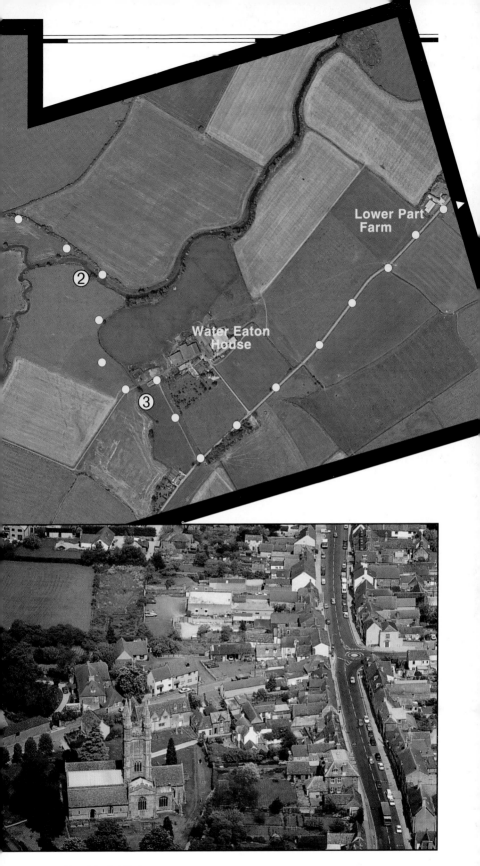

Lower Part Farm

Water Eaton House

St Sampson's Church in Cricklade

ROUTE DIRECTIONS

1. On the far side of the river turn right and follow the path up the hill, roughly parallel to the river, crossing two fields. Bear half-right on entering a third field. This brings you back to the Thames which is recrossed at Water Eaton footbridge.
2. Go straight ahead, with a ditch on your left, and cross a stile. Go through another gate and turn left on to the farm track, heading towards the barns for 100yds.
3. Turn right through another gate on to a clear track with a hedge on your left and reach the road. Turn left on to the road and continue past Lower Part Farm.

CASTLE EATON IS a quaint little village beside the Thames, compact and delightful. The castle was a stronghold of the Zouche family during Norman times but today there is no sign of it. However, the church down by the river has two Norman doorways, one of which is carved with watchful dragons, and a Norman font carved with flowers.

The church was restored in 1861-3 and the corbelled bell-turret and spire added. The bell is undeniably from the 14th century, and is thought to be the original sanctus bell. It was discovered in 1900 and set into the bell-turret.

Across the river beyond Kempsford is Fairford, where Royalist troops were garrisoned during the Civil War, and massive RAF Fairford. This airfield has a runway nearly 2 miles (3.2km) long and was used for testing 'Concorde'. During Word War II it was important in the deployment of parachute troops for airborne invasions over the Continent. More recently it became a USAF base and their huge tanker-aircraft still use it.

ROUTE DIRECTIONS

1. Continue along the lane and turn left at the road junction into The Street.
2. Pass Castle Eaton Farm, the Red Lion pub and the lychgate entrance to the church and bear right with the road into Long Row.
3. Turn left into School Lane. Bear right with the road and turn left along Blackford Lane towards Blackford Farm (views to Kempsford on the right over the Thames).

②

③

**CASTLE
EATON**

*Fairford, over 3 miles (4.8km) north of Castle
Eaton on the River Coln, is another pleasant
Cotswold town*

Kempsford

CASTLE
EATON

N

ROUTE DIRECTIONS

1. Continue along the lane to Blackford Farm. Walk between Forty Acre Barn and Blackford Farm on to the line of a footpath, and straight across the field. Go over the plank bridge across a ditch to cross a stile into the next field. Bear gently to the left over the next field and cross the plank.
2. Bear left to walk alongside a watercourse.

KEMPSFORD, ACCORDING TO tradition, was a stronghold of the Saxon kings of Mercia. It faced Wessex across the river, which formed the boundary between the two, although it was possible to ford it here. A nearby 100-acre (40ha) meadow is still known as Battlefield after a Saxon skirmish. This part of the walk keeps company with the great tower of Kempsford church, visible on the far side of the Thames. This was built by one of history's great names, John of Gaunt, Duke of Lancaster, uncle to Richard II and father of Henry IV. He raised the tower 600 years ago in memory of his wife, Lady Blanche (patroness of Geoffrey Chaucer), who died aged 29 in 1369. At Kempsford we meet with the first of the Thames ghosts, that of Lady Maud, the beautiful young shade who forever haunts the broad riverside terrace known as Lady Maud's Walk. This terrace is much older than the ghost, for it formed part of the Saxon defences, but has been faced with more modern masonry. Lady Maud was either Lady Blanche's sister or her grandmother – tradition is somewhat misty in this respect – and she was married to one of the barons who opposed the king during the turbulent civil wars that ended the reign of either Richard II or Edward II. Lady Maud, who was living at Kempsford, helped those of her husband's followers who sought refuge there. Among the fugitives was her husband's brother whom, as he had a price on his head, she hid secretly at the end of the long terrace overlooking the Thames. Morning and evening she would creep along the terrace to take him his food, arousing the suspicions of one of her husband's retinue, who begged him to return and witness Maud's infidelity. So it was that in a rage the earl attacked his own brother and flung his innocent wife into the Thames. Since then she has haunted the spot.

In 1549 Kempsford manor was bought by Sir John Thynne whose descendants demolished the old house and, during the reign of James I, built a large mansion. This in turn was demolished, much of the stone being shipped down the Thames to Buscot. Later, the manor of Kempsford passed into the hands of the Lords Coleraine.

Sir John Betjeman told a fine story of an Irish peer who ended up buried in the organ. The truth behind this tale originated in Kempsford, the unfortunate Irishman being the 3rd Lord Coleraine. He died in 1814 and was buried in Kempsford church, but some 50 years later the organ was built on top of his tomb.

The Thames and Severn Canal passed through Kempsford, though it is now difficult to trace its route. At one time there was a wharf here, commemorated in Wharf Cottages.

KEMPSFORD

Blackford Farm

②

HANNINGTON WICK

HANNINGTON BRIDGE IS on the site of a Roman crossing and there are further Roman relics here. To the south of the clump of trees that mark the site of vanished Sterts Farm, between the former farmstead and the hill on which Highworth stands, are a series of circular earthworks, with diameters of between 80yds and 100yds. Built during the Roman occupation, they seem to be associated with the British farms of that period. Their actual purpose – either cattle shelters or homesteads – remains unknown.

The now derelict Thames and Severn Canal has shadowed the Thames since the source. Lying to the north of the river, it was built to link the Thames waterway and the eastern ports of the country with the River Severn and the western ports. It ran for about 30 miles (48km), from near Lechlade to Stroud. Construction was on a large scale and the canal was heavily locked in order to climb up and over the watershed; at the western end it had to climb 250ft (76m) using 28 locks, whereupon it fell 135ft (41m) in 14 locks. However, these were dwarfed by the 4,300-yds long Sapperton tunnel, the longest canal tunnel in Britain and one of the wonders of the age. In his comprehensive survey of British canals, published in 1831, Joseph Priestley says that:

On the 19th July 1778, during the execution of this work, his late majesty, King George III went to view the tunnel, with which he expressed himself much astonished, and on the construction of which he bestowed the highest praise...

The canal was opened in 1789 at the height of the canal age. However, the hopes of a lucrative return for the shareholders were not realised, and a contemporary of Priestley had to report to his readers that '...we fear these anticipations have not lately been realised, as the amount of the dividend has now become extremely limited...'.

There were a number of reasons why the canal did not prosper. For one, it suffered from chronic water shortages and the upper reach of the Thames, beyond Oxford, remained a difficult navigation for barge traffic. Later, the North Wiltshire Canal was built to avoid the upper Thames, but it was too late, and with the coming of the nearby railway the canal fell into disuse towards the end of the 1890s. An attempt by a Gloucestershire count was made around that time to revive the canal, but

HANNINGTON
WICK

A view back over Kempsford and Fairford Airfield

although this proved futile it was not abandoned until 1927. Sadly, there does not appear to be any likelihood of this fascinating canal being restored.

ROUTE DIRECTIONS

1. Continue alongside the watercourse crossing two more stiles to reach the road near Hannington Bridge.
2. Turn right past Bridge Farm, then left following the bridleway sign on to a lane.
3. Bear right on to the grassy track and carry on through the gate on to a bridleway with a stream and a hedge on your left.
4. Walk along the bridleway bearing left round a woodland (site of Sterts Farm) and continue along the grassy track to a small belt of woodland. Go through the gate bearing right beside an old ford to cross the footbridge over a small stream.

INGLESHAM

UPPER
INGLESHAM

THERE ARE TWO INGLESHAMS, Upper and Lower. The former is the present-day village, situated on a hilltop above the river with views across pleasant Cotswold country. The latter is a tiny place beside the Thames which has dwindled from being a flourishing wool village. It has an 11th-century church – a former priory chapel that was beautifully restored 100 years ago. There is an inscription which reads 'This church was repaired in 1888-9 through the energy and with the help of William Morris, who loved it'.

The late Anglo-Saxon sculpture of Virgin and Child with the hand of God is strangely moving and unconventional. The iconography could derive from Northumbrian 7th-century sources such as St Cuthbert's coffin and the *Book of Kells*. The nave is Anglo-Saxon in origin, while the chancel is 13th-century, as is the double bellcote. There are wall paintings of all ages, mostly superimposed, so that the individual paintings appear as scraps on the walls. The pulpit and box pews are Jacobean.

The Thames and Severn Canal joined the Thames at Inglesham close to the confluence of the Thames and its tributary the Coln. Inglesham Lock stood at that point. It is now in the private garden of the Round House, a former lock-keeper's cottage which consists of a creeper-clad tower with later extensions.

ROUTE DIRECTIONS

1. Bear right through the trees and follow the bridleway through the fields. Turn left on to a lane into Upper Inglesham.
2. Follow the lane to the main road (A361) and turn left. This road is dangerous, so take extreme care.
3. Turn left down the lane signed to Inglesham church then turn right through the gate before Inglesham House to head down to the Thames across a field scarred by the humps and hollows of the deserted medieval village of Inglesham.
4. Bear right to reach the Thames and cross the metal bridge over a small tributary stream.

5. Follow the path along the river bank which shortly joins the Thames towpath at the footbridge opposite the confluence of the River Coln and the ruined Thames and Severn Canal.

The approach to Lechlade from Inglesham

Lechlade to Tadpole Bridge

10 ½ miles (16.75km)

From Lechlade downstream the Thames is a navigable waterway, and where possible the Thames Path uses the towpath. Originally a commercial waterway, the river is now the haunt of pleasure launches and all manner of craft. It winds between wide open meadows of waving grass, and between October and April, when the motor cruisers are laid up, the walker can feel remote and free as the sweeping winds. Lechlade and Kelmscot have literary associations, while Radcot witnessed a medieval skirmish which changed the course of history.

LECHLADE TAKES ITS name from the little River Leach which joins the Thames at St John's Bridge. The spire of its church, St Lawrence's, one of the great wool churches of the Cotswolds, is visible for miles around. This church, built in 1474, is perpendicular in its entirety, with no trace of the earlier building remaining.

Halfpenny Bridge, complete with its toll house, replaced the ferry in 1792. It was built by the townsfolk and the toll for pedestrians was a halfpenny, thus christening the bridge. Horses were charged twopence and carriages sixpence.

In 1815 the rebel poet, Shelley, stayed at Lechlade with Thomas Love Peacock (author of the poem 'The Genius of the Thames'), Mary Godwin and Charles Clairmont. Wandering beneath the yews and copper beeches in the churchyard on a summer evening, the sight of the lofty spire inspired him to write: 'Thou, too, aerial pile, whose pinnacle Point from one shrine like pyramids of fire ...'.

The busy little wharf at Lechlade now sees only pleasure traffic, but 200 years ago it was alive with commercial barges. St John's Lock is the highest lock on the river and is modest compared to the giants lower down. Beside it today is a reclining statue of Neptune bearing aloft, not the expected trident, but a paddle. This is Father Thames, sculpted for the Great Exhibition of 1851. In 1958 he was acquired by one of the Thames Conservators and set up in Trewsbury Mead but vandals attacked him and he was surrounded by railings. Then, in 1974, to prevent further damage, he was moved to his present position.

The present St John's Bridge dates from 1831, with alterations of 1884, but there has been a bridge here for a long while as records of grants for repairs stretching back to the 14th century show. At the northern end of the bridge, where the Trout pub now stands, was the priory of St John Baptist, set up in 1246 to tend the sick. King John granted local fishing rights to the priors, and these now belong to the Trout.

BUSCOT LOCK, the next downstream from St John's, had a new weir built in 1979. Buscot Park, the large mansion on the hill about a mile to the south, was built in about 1780 using materials carried down the Thames from the demolished manor at Kempsford.

Buscot village (National Trust), on the south side of the river, was built as a model village in 1879 by Squire Campbell, an Australian who had bought the Buscot Estate. He virtually ruined himself in his attempts to introduce modern farming methods, bringing hundreds of acres under cultivation for sugar beet. Steam ploughs worked day and night, lit by great limelights, and the sugar beet went to the distillery near the lock to produce alcohol. An Act of Parliament allowed the squire to build a riverside pumping station with a waterwheel 16ft (4.8m) wide which weighed 25 tons. This was situated in the mill stream near the old lock-keeper's cottage; it not only irrigated his lands but supplied his tenants with water.

Campbell sold out to Alexander Henderson, later Lord Faringdon, whose son, the 2nd Lord, was an eccentric socialist, pacifist peer. His son, the 3rd Lord, still lives at Buscot Park. Between Buscot and Kelmscot is the site of Hart's Weir (or Eaton Weir), marked today by a footbridge. Here, until 1936, was the last of the flashlocks on the navigable river. During the 1830s the lock-keeper was a Mr Hart who was involved in smuggling and hid kegs of contraband spirits, which had come up-river by barge, on long chains at the bottom of the river. The former lock-keeper's house became an inn, the Angler, which burnt down some years ago.

Kelmscot is forever associated with the Pre-Raphaelites, especially William Morris who made his home at Kelmscot Manor in 1871 and is buried in the churchyard. Morris later described the manor house as 'A heaven on earth.... an old Elizabethan house, like Water Eaton, and such a garden, close down on the river'. The house was built in 1570 and a north wing added in 1670.

Of a June day at Kelmscot Morris wrote: '...What better place than this, then, could we find, By this sweet stream that knows not of the sea, That guesses not the city's misery, This little stream whose hamlets scarce have names, This-far off, lonely mother of the Thames.'

Rossetti, who originally shared the Kelmscot lease with Morris, lived here too in 1871. He pursued Morris's wife, Janey, found that his temperament and that of his friend were utterly incompatible, and alienated the locals. He complained that the village of muted grey stone set deep among its trees was '...the doziest dump of old grey beehives...'. Eventually he left, but Morris lived here and loved the place for 25 years.

Morris was a remarkable man; artist, designer, printer, poet, writer and political thinker. Kelmscot is the 'Nowhere' in Morris's *News From Nowhere*.

A footpath leads south from the Thames Path to the National Trust property of Buscot House

KELMSCOT

ROUTE DIRECTIONS

1. Turn right at Buscot, crossing over the large new weir and then turn left at Buscot Lock, going across the green with the river on your left. Go through the gate and follow the path over the grass. Turn left to cross back over the Thames by the concrete bridge. **2.** Carry on along the towpath with the river on your right, past Eaton weir footbridge and on to Kelmscot.

ST MICHAEL'S CHURCH and the few buildings seen across the river at Eaton Hastings mark the position of a vanished village. This was situated on the gravel river terrace.

Grafton Lock was formerly known as Day's Weir, or Lower Hart's Weir, and from the 1780s right up to 1821, or there-abouts, was owned by Mrs Hart of Hart's (or Eaton) Weir and her son. At that time the Thames was a very important commercial highway, and part of the great system of inland waterways which preceded the railways as a means of transport of merchandise. Improvements to the Thames in the name of navigation started early. Weirs, created by millers to provide a head of water for their watermills, conflicted with the use of the Thames for river traffic. Boats would have to shoot the weir, leading to arguments between the millers and the bargemen. The next development was weirs in which a part could be lifted (the flashlock), so that boats could pass down in the flash of water, although boats going up would have to be hauled against the current. These gave way in the 1790s to separate weirs with the familiar poundlocks although the last flashlock did not disap-pear until 1936.

The mixed merchandise carried by the river barges, towed by gangs of men (halers) or by horses, who tramped along the towpath we tread today, included nails, cheese, raw hides, artillery shells and cannons.

Many of today's riverside resorts were important inland ports and this was especially true of Lechlade, where as many as 100 barges would moor between Halfpenny Bridge and St John's Lock. Many of these barges were involved in shifting stone from Taynton Quarries, near Burford, down to London to build St Paul's Cathedral, while the single most important merchandise shipped from Lechlade was Gloucester cheese, 3,000 tons of which was handled per annum at the end of the 17th century. The stretch of towpath between Kelmscot and Radcot is haunted by another Thames-side ghost, the Headless Boatman. His tale is soon told: some time during the 1500s there lived in Kelmscot a man who is known locally only as the boatman. One day, at Radcot, he was accused of sheep-stealing, and the farmer whose sheep had disappeared took the law into his own hands and struck off the boatman's head with a butcher's cleaver. Since that day the boatman's ghost haunts the river bank, heading back home to Kelmscot looking for justice.

EATON HASTINGS

Great Barn (National Trust), near Bradbury Hill, south of the Thames

ROUTE DIRECTIONS

1. At Kelmscot cross the footbridge over a stream and bear right on to the track to keep to the river bank along the towpath (or, if you wish, you can bear left into the little hamlet).

2. Keep going along the towpath, with the lonely church of Eaton Hastings on the opposite bank, till you come to Grafton Lock. Go through the gate and across the grass and out by the next gate.

3 Continue along the towpath, with the river on your right.

RADCOT CONSISTS OF an inn and two bridges, two because a cut was made here in 1787 to ease out a meander bend for the increased traffic expected on the new Thames and Severn Canal. Thus a little island has been created, which has become popular with boating and camping fraternities. The old bridge is probably the oldest over the Thames, dating from about 1280, though a Saxon charter suggests that there was a bridge here as early as AD958. The new bridge over the navigation channel was built in 1787. Beside it, where now are the gardens of the Swan Inn, was an important wharf for the shipment of Taynton stone for building in London. This replaced an earlier wharf from which the stone was shipped the 26 miles (41.6km) to Oxford for the building of many of the older colleges.

The old bridge possesses three arches, the two outer ones pointed, the central one rounded, for early on in its life it had to be rebuilt. In 1387 the country was in open conflict with Richard II, but the Earl of Oxford declared for him and, with an army of 5,000 men, marched to Radcot to cut off the pretender to the throne, Henry Bolingbroke. Henry had anticipated Oxford's arrival and shattered the central arch of the bridge, thus trapping his enemy between his own troops and the swift-flowing river, so that they were either taken by surprise or drowned. Oxford himself plunged into the Thames to escape and went into exile. The engagement at Radcot Bridge changed the course of English history, for the King was forced to come to terms with Henry. However, it was not until 1399 that Richard II was finally overthrown and died in captivity, when Bolingbroke became Henry IV. There was another skirmish at Radcot in 1645 during the great Civil War, when it held out for Charles I. Prince Rupert's men, serving as an outpost to the Royalist stronghold at Faringdon, camped on Garrison Field and fought off the Parliamentarians. Radcot Lock occupies the site off an old flashweir. It was known by a variety of names, including Clarke's Weir, named after the one-time weir keeper.

Uninterrupted views over farmland are very much a feature of these early stages of the walk

RADCOT

③

ROUTE DIRECTIONS

1. Continue to Radcot, where the Thames occupies two channels. Turn right to cross the bridge over the northerly channel (the modern navigation channel). Once over the bridge turn left through a gate and walk along the right-hand bank of this channel (medieval Radcot Bridge is on your right).

2. Cross the former main stream by the wooden bridge and continue along the towpath to Radcot Lock.

3. Go through the gate and along the strip of grass past the lock on to a Conservancy road. Go through another gateback on to the towpath and carry on past Old Man's footbridge.

RUSHEY IS FIRST mentioned in September 1542 in connection with a grant of 'the several water called Rushey, flowing within the parish of Bampton...' to Robert Kyng, Bishop of Oxford. Rushey Lock opened in winter 1790, and its first keeper is named as a Mr Rudge. That important documenter of the Thames in the early 20th century, Fred Thacker, speaks affectionately in his *Stripling Thames* of Tom Weal of Rushey Lock. The view north is dominated by a forest of radio masts and the elegant spire of Bampton's parish church. Until the 18th century this spire used to guide travellers to the little grey-stone market town, for Bampton was not served by any roads. In fact, its old name of Bampton-in-the-Bush recalls this isolation, though it was mentioned as long ago as Domesday, in 1086. It rose to prominence as a market town in the 18th century and today is known chiefly for its Whit Monday carnival. This is first and foremost the day of the Morris dancers, for two teams, clad in white and tinkling with bells, take to the streets. A plum cake is carried around the town, impaled on a sword, and the crowd are encouraged to buy pieces – which are said to bring good luck.

Faringdon lies to the south, its position marked by a clump of trees which surround Faringdon Folly, a narrow, brick tower built in 1936 by the 14th Lord Berners, owner of Faringdon House.

Old Man's footbridge is on the site of Old Man's Weir. Just downstream there used to be an Old Nan's Weir too, but this has disappeared entirely.

There is little riverside habitation here because of the former existence of a marshland tract which proved a great hindrance to the development of the area. Until it had been drained this lowland clay vale was not only very difficult to cross, but also generally unsuitable for building. Moreover, the river here formed a natural boundary from earliest times. During Saxon times it was the boundary between Wessex and Mercia. Until 1974 it also was the boundary between Berkshire and Oxfordshire. And, as the pillboxes along the left-hand bank go to show, it would have been a boundary for that battle that never was, if, in 1940, the German army had invaded successfully. The upper Thames was the obvious defensive line and, even if there had not been fighting in the immediate vicinity, the bridges would have been blown up as a matter of course.

**Rushey
Lock**

②

N

ROUTE DIRECTIONS

1. Carry on along the towpath beside the meandering river to reach the weir at Rushey Lock.
2. Turn left over the weir and then turn right to take the path through the garden of the lock cottage. Walk alongside the lock and cross the lower lock gates. Go through the gate back to the banks of the Thames and continue downstream, with the river on your right.

Old Smokedown Cottages, south of Old Man's footbridge

Tadpole Bridge to Bablock Hythe

10¼ miles (16.5km)

This section of the walk hardly touches human settlement.
The old towpath is somewhat overgrown in places and the
walk beside the Thames is conducted in solitude, apart from
the cattle in the wide meadows and the pleasure-boats
plying the river. Having left the Trout Inn at Tadpole, habitation consists only of the two inns at Newbridge (a misnomer,
for it is the second oldest bridge over the river), the little
hamlet of Duxford and the lock at Northmoor, before
reaching Bablock Hythe.

ROUTE DIRECTIONS

1. Continue along the towpath and through the gate on to
the road near the Trout Inn at Tadpole Bridge.
2. Cross the road and go through the gate and down the
steps on the farther side of Tadpole Bridge. Continue
along the towpath with the Thames on your right.
3. Follow the towpath, which is badly overgrown, along the
top of the river bank, crossing several stiles before
reaching Tenfoot Bridge.

N

TADPOLE

TADPOLE BRIDGE IS first referenced on Robert Whitworth's map of 1784 and by 1796 there was discussion of 'a new bridge at Tadpole'. The present bridge was built in 1802. Below it there was quite a considerable coal wharf, now used as moorings for pleasure craft. There was also a weir at Tadpole, known variously as Tadpole, Rudge's or Kent's Weir. It seems that in 1802 a Mrs Kent was responsible for Duxford Weir 3 miles (5km) downstream, and may also have been in charge. However, the weir was removed in 1869 and by 1875 local farmers were requesting its replacement, citing flood damage to their crops and claiming compensation from the Thames Conservancy.

The small village of Buckland lies about a mile south of Tadpole and Buckland House, family seat of the great Throckmorton family, is an exceptionally imposing 18th-century building. It was built in 1757 by John Ward the younger, but is not open to the public.

Along the banks of the Thames are some interesting pollard willows. Pollarding is an ancient type of woodland management which relies on the fact that many trees grow again from a stump. Pollards are cut some 6-10ft (1.8-3m) above ground level so that cattle will not feed on the new shoots and destroy them (this compares with coppicing, in which the tree is cut to ground level). Pollard willows are fast-growing though short-lived, and produce a useful crop of branches to make small stakes, hurdles, baskets and firewood if cropped every six or seven years. The practice of growing them along river banks probably began during the 13th century and was an important source of wood along this stretch of the Thames. Moreover, the trees help to maintain the river banks as their roots bind the soil and prevent erosion. Sadly, many of these Thames-side pollards are dying, and the cropping of the trees is becoming uneconomical.

Pusey House (not open) and its tiny hamlet can be reached from Tenfoot Bridge via Buckland

N

THE STRANGE NAME of Tenfoot Bridge relates to a now forgotten weir with a 10-ft (3m) flash opening for the traffic. The weir was removed in 1869 when the bridge was built and the waterway widened. Shifford Lock and cut were made in 1898, and the natural Thames channel which loops south past Duxford was bypassed. It has become a delightful backwater. Here is the last true ford on the Thames: the only one not to have been replaced by a bridge and a lock. Today, its concrete base is partly broken and the water flowing swiftly over the sill is deeper than it should be.

Chimney is a small hamlet set on a gravel river terrace to the north of the river, really consisting of no more than a farmhouse and a couple of labourers' cottages. From the towpath this part of the Thames valley seems to be utterly empty: the only houses are by the locks and the bridges, and the only villages some way off, their existence marked by a tell-tale spire or the masts of a radio-station. There are few hedges, some pollard willows and a rich meadowland of grazing herds interspersed by clumps of hawthorn and tangles of bramble. The river meanders at will across a flat plain which betrays its past as a marshland by deep drainage ditches, the banks broken down where cattle have come to drink. In winter, when there is hardly any river

traffic, this is a lonely reach indeed.

The birdlife associated with the Thames makes use of the differing habitats found along it. Fish-eating birds are common, especially herons which can be seen all along the river. Where willows and alders overhang the water they provide suitable perches for kingfishers, especially in the upper reaches of the river, and their seeds are fed upon in winter by flocks of siskins and redpolls. Moorhens and coots are frequently seen amid vegetation on the banks, particularly where there are undisturbed backwaters. There are many species of duck, including mallard, pochard and teal, augmented in winter by migrants such as goldeneye. These breed on reservoirs and flooded gravel pits near the river, which they visit frequently. Mute swans are increasing in numbers since the use of lead weights by anglers was banned in 1987.

ROUTE DIRECTIONS

1. Turn right across Tenfoot Bridge and go straight on along the track that leads away from the river. Turn left along a bridleway, with a ditch on your right.

2. Turn right just beyond the pylon and continue till you come to a gap in the hedge on your left. Turn left through this gap.

3. Bear right around the field to the opposite side. Go through the gap and continue with the hedge on your right. Cross the footbridge to reach Duxford Farm.

4. Carry on past the farm on to a little lane, beneath poplar trees, which bears to the right and then to the left. Just as the lane is about to swing to the right again bear left on to a track by a thatched cottage.

5. Go down this track, which narrows to a path, to the ford on the old river channel and then bear right to join the path on the top of the river bank.

6. Continue along this overgrown path till you come to the weir at Shifford Lock cut, going through three broken-down gates along the way.

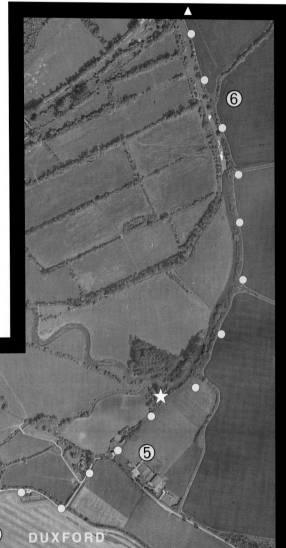

Swans and Canada geese are frequently seen grazing on the watermeadows in winter.

Mammals are not numerous along the Thames. The effects of river traffic and the constant trampling of the banks by anglers and walkers have led to a paucity of suitable habitats. Otters are virtually unknown now, but water voles (often known as water rats) are found, and can sometimes be seen swimming in the river.

SHIFFORD

Shifford
Lock

①

Hinton Waldrist (shown here) and its neighbour Longworth overlook the valley from the south

SHIFFORD, ON THE north bank, stands lonely and remote in its great meadows. This, like Inglesham and Eaton Hastings, is a dwindled remnant of a once important place. Indeed, Shifford was once a royal borough. A piece of ground near the church is known as Court Close, and here, according to tradition, Alfred the Great held one of the first English parliaments.

The old chroniclers say: '...There sat at Shiffordd many thanes, many bishops, and many learned men, wise earls and awful knights ... and Alfred, England's herdsman, England's darling; he was king of England; he taught them that could hear him how they should live ...'.

ROUTE DIRECTIONS

1. Continue downstream along the path with the river on your left. On the opposite bank you pass Old Shifford Farm, virtually all that remains of a substantial deserted village.

ABOUT A MILE AND A HALF downstream of Shifford Lock is the site of an old ford, Sansom's or Samson's. In another half mile are the faint traces of Limbre's Weir, under the slopes of Harrow down Hill. Known in 1796 as Townsend's Weir, or Langley's, it was rented by Thomas Hart, making it the third weir so far associated with the Harts, a great river family. In 1802 it seems to have been rather neglected, apparently in favour of good fishing rather than good navigation. By 1832, although described as 'picturesquely situated', it was nonetheless regarded as 'dangerous, without due caution, to small boats'.

Standlake, about a mile north of Newbridge, is built along a line of dykes on land reclaimed from the river. The Church of St Giles, with its 14th-century tower, was restored in 1880-91 and has life-size angels in the roof. Gaunt House is on a moated site and during the Civil War was fortified for the king. The woodwork of one of the doors is peppered with little holes – evidence of musket-shots.

Newbridge, where the River Windrush flows into the Thames, is regarded as the oldest bridge on the river after Radcot. It was built by the Pontific Brothers, Benedictine monks from the nearby priory at La Nore (Northmoor), probably about the year 1250. The stone, from the Taynton quarries, was brought down the Windrush to this point. The bridge, which consists of six pointed arches, is well known for its two inns. On the right-hand bank is the Maybush, and on the left-hand bank the Rose Revived – a name resulting from the imagination of a new landlord. The inn was originally the Rose and later the Crown, but he resisted the temptation of renaming it the Rose and Crown and reverted to the older name.

Leland, the 16th-century topographer, described the area around Newbridge as 'a fair champain ground fruitful of corn ... the ground there all about lieth in low meadows and often overflows by rage of rain'. Causeways approach the bridge from both the north and the south, raising the road above the low-lying land subject to flooding. It was substantially rebuilt in the 15th century and again repaired in 1801.

There was a skirmish at Newbridge on 1 June 1644 during the Civil War.

Harrowdown Hill between Shifford and Newbridge

ROUTE DIRECTIONS

1. Carry on along this overgrown path, keeping close to the river, till you arrive at Newbridge at the confluence of the Thames and the River Windrush.

2. Go through the gate and over the footbridge to skirt the garden of the Maybush pub. Turn left here to cross over stately stone Newbridge.

3. Turn right on the opposite bank and go through the garden of the Rose Revived inn. Continue along the towpath with the river on your right.

ABOUT A MILE below Newbridge, where now there is only Hart's footbridge, there was another Hart's Weir – but it was removed in 1880.

During the 18th century the weir keeper at Hart's Weir was a Mr Rudge. His daughter, Betty, by all accounts a sweet and gentle girl, helped him with the ferry. One day a student from Christ Church came here to fish – surely no rare occurrence – and he and Betty fell in love. However, in those days of rigid class barriers, one would expect the story to have a sad ending, for the student was none other than the 2nd Viscount Ashbrook, and any honourable association with one of Betty's class would have been out of the question. The young peer, however, was not daunted, proposed marriage, was accepted and sent Betty to some nearby gentlefolk to be taught the social graces. They were married in Northmoor church in 1766 and were blissfully happy for the 18 years of their married life. Betty married again, 10 years after the Viscount's death, and herself died in 1808, 'much loved and respected'.

Northmoor Lock was constructed in 1895 to replace the old Hart's, or Rudge's weir – a new structure entirely – although it is worked not by sluices but by the old-fashioned paddles and rhymers. The former Ark Weir (or yet another Hart's Weir), which stood 3 miles (4.8km) below Newbridge was also known as Noah's Ark. This weir was described as a bustling scene by Boydell in 1794, but by 1851 it had 'gone to decay'. In 1884 this old weir site is mentioned as 'A very small extent of fishery, belonging now to a man named William Hart, who has deeds going back to 1745; and this family have got their living from that piece of fishery from that time to the present'.

Northmoor Lock

②

ROUTE DIRECTIONS

1. Carry on along the towpath, past Hart's footbridge, to Northmoor Lock. Go through the gates and past the lock cottage.
2. Continue along the towpath.

Kingston House, about 3 miles (4.8km) due south of Newbridge, is open on certain days in the summer

Bablock Hythe to Oxford (Osney Bridge)

10½ miles (16.75km)

This section starts by following field paths and returns to the river at Pinkhill. After a tiny stretch on the road where the towpath has fallen into the river the walk continues along the grassy towpath into Wytham Great Wood and round the great meander to head south again to Godstow with the sadly meagre remains of its once great nunnery. Then it's down alongside great unenclosed Port Meadow and behind the backs of houses to emerge at Osney Bridge in urban Oxford.

BABLOCK HYTHE IS mentioned in Matthew Arnold's great poem, 'The Scholar Gipsy', the tale of an erstwhile Oxford student who '...Tired of knocking at Preferment's door', joined the vagabonds and lived a gipsy life. The tale of this half-mythical figure, lifted by Arnold from a 17th-century tract, caught the imagination of those who, like him, regretted the 'march of industrial Britain with its attendant ugliness of form and spirit, the sick disease of modern life'.

Places around Oxford are magically evoked in the poem, and its successor, 'Thyrsis', so it is that the 'lost scholar' is seen at the ferry by a group of revellers returning to Oxford, 'Crossing the stripling Thames at Bablock-Hythe'.

There has been a crossing here from time immemorial; first there was a ford, stretching back at least to the Romans, and then a ferry. In AD948 the place was a major river port known as Babballacu-Hyth, 'the landing place by Babba's stream'. In 1320 the ferryman was John le Keu, while a manuscript of 1692 comments that 'Bablock Hythe has a great boat to carry over Carts & Coaches'.

Over the years the ferry became more sophisticated and during World War II the vehicle ferry here was kept busy by army convoys. However, the traffic dwindled and in 1986 the ferry ceased to operate. The Ferryman Inn shut down too, but it has now reopened and the landlord runs a small ferry – a rowing boat – thus reinstating a 1,000-year-old tradition.

There is another tradition here that is worth the telling, redolent with humanity's age-old fascination with river deities. It is said that if you throw four coins into the Thames from the Bablock Hythe ferry, it will be returned to you sevenfold.

Opposite us at Bablock Hythe are wooded slopes, the 'warm, green-muffled Cumnor Hills...' of which Matthew Arnold wrote. The old village of Cumnor nestles among them, invisible from the river. But it was here that Amy Robstart, wife of Elizabeth I's favourite, Robert Dudley, was found dead at the bottom of the stairs of Cumnor Place. Was it murder, simply a tragic accident, or even suicide? The old house has vanished, but the memory remains, shrouded in mystery. Some of Amy's letters are kept in the church.

ROUTE DIRECTIONS

1. Follow the towpath till you reach the Ferry-man Inn at Bablock Hythe.
2. Turn left away from the river and walk along the road before turning right along a bridleway with a hedge on your left.

Bablock Hythe with the Ferryman inn

ROUTE DIRECTIONS

1. Continue along the bridleway and turn right when you come to a meeting of bridleways and then left over a stile. Follow the path obliquely across two fields.

2. Cross the footbridge in the corner of the field and continue across the meadow to the river bank.

3. Follow the path with the river on your right till you come to Pinkhill Lock.

4. Cross the weir and follow the path through the grass to cross the lock over the upper gates.

5. Turn left out of the lock and follow the towpath with the river on your left. Cross a footbridge and turn to the right away from the river up a path to the B4044.

6. Turn left along the pavement beside the road and then left again down the private road to Oxford Cruisers Boatyard. Turn right just before the blue footbridge over a little dock to regain the towpath with the river on your left.

The church and Pope's Tower in Stanton Harcourt

THE VILLAGE OF Stanton Harcourt stands on a gravel terrace to the left of the Thames Path and was, until 1711, when they moved to Nuneham Courtenay, the seat of the Harcourt family. Two towers rise above the trees. One belongs to the church, the other is virtually all that remains of a great mansion demolished in about 1750. It is known as Pope's Tower, for here, in 1718, while the house was falling into decay, the poet, Alexander Pope spent the summer on his famous translation of Homer's *Iliad*. Notwithstanding the demolition of most of the mansion, the remains are impressive and include what must be the most spectacular medieval domestic kitchen in England. They are maintained as a private home, but are open to the public.

The dignified 13th-century church is full of great monuments to the Harcourts, including one to Robert Harcourt, his tomb effigy resplendent in armour. He was standard bearer to Henry Tudor at the Battle of Bosworth, where that doughty Welshman is said to have found the crown of England on a thorn bush. The first Viscount Harcourt and his son, Simon, have an epitaph by Alexander Pope. So do the unfortunate rustic lovers, John Hewet and Sarah Drew who were 'both in one instant killed by lightning on the last day of July 1718'. This incident affected Pope deeply. Another monument is to Sir William Harcourt, whose claim to fame is that he introduced graduated death duties. He died in 1904, ten years before world war sent taxes spiralling inexorably upwards!

Farmoor Reservoir, across the river from Stanton Harcourt, has a surface area of 380 acres (154ha) and is hidden behind its grassy bank. It draws water from the Thames and supplies water to a large part of Oxfordshire. In times of drought, water from the reservoir is used to top up the river level. It is popular with dinghy sailors, trout fishers and ornithologists.

The path rejoins the Thames at the site of the former Skinner's Weir. The modern channel which turns off to the right is a cut made in 1896-99. Here there was a mill and an attendant inn, the Fish. It is now a delightfully sylvan spot. Skinner's Weir and the Fish were mentioned thus in 1797: 'On a small island, planted with fruit trees, a thatched cottage offers repose and refreshment'. Later, it was described as '... a little inn; and the last landlord, Joe Skinner, was one of the best hearted, quaintest fellows that ever lived. He was original to the highest degree, and it was a rich treat to listen to his curious remarks ...'. The weir fell into disrepair, and in July 1880 it gave way.

Pinkhill Lock is a mile below old Skinner's, down the twisting turning river. The poundlock was built in 1791, and partially rebuilt in 1877. A cut was excavated in 1899 to take flood water. In 1909 Mr H. Smith was appointed lock keeper. He cleared the lock island of its vegetation and won the prize in 1910 for the best kept lock on the whole river. Thacker was rather unsure if the clearance was a good thing, for he wrote with affection of '... the rambling wilderness of a garden, full of vegetable patches and familiar old world flowers, crowded in summer with scores of campers...'.

BEACON HILL, behind Pinkhill Lock, is one of the ragstone hills of the Oxford Heights. It was christened in 1588 when it was fired in that great chain of beacons lit across the land to tell all England that the Spanish Armada had been sighted in the Channel.

Swinford Bridge was built by the Earl of Abingdon in 1777 as part of a turnpike road, and replaced a ferry. It is one of only two toll bridges remaining on the Thames and the charge has to remain at an old penny a wheel, so cars cross for 2p!

Eynsham Lock sits just beyond the bridge. In 1791 the weir here was owned by Lord Abingdon, but by 1795 it was so decayed that he was ordered to collect no more tolls till he had repaired it. Even in 1859 the passage is described as 'somewhat dangerous'.

ROUTE DIRECTIONS

1. Continue along the towpath with the river on your right and go over a stile. Carry on and follow the towpath under the arches of Swinford Bridge. (Eynsham is across the bridge to the left.)

2. Continue beyond the bridge to Eynsham Lock. Beyond the lock the path bears left over a footbridge. Carry on along the towpath through the edge of Wytham Great Wood (owned by Oxford University) which here comes down to the Thames. Farther on an old canal and the River Evenlode join the Thames on the opposite side.

Swinford Bridge and Eynsham Lock

THE WEIR AT KING'S LOCK is
mentioned in 1541 with regard to a grant
of land. In 1791 it seems to have been in
the hands of the Duke of Marlborough,
who never collected any tolls, and by
1802 it was in ruins. It must have been
rebuilt, however, for in 1813 we find one
of the Harts in charge here. There were
constant demands for a lock and one
was eventually constructed in 1928!
Duke's Cut was built here privately in
1789 by the Duke of Marlborough to link
the upper Thames to the brand new
Oxford Canal. Although this cut was
independent, it was later leased to the
canal company in 1798 for 200 years. The
lock connecting the river with the
Oxford Canal is interesting, being
constructed so as to give a fall either
way, according to which navigation has,
for the time being, the higher level. This
design of lock is invariably used for
docks where the tidal range is
considerable, but is very rare inland.

The Oxford Canal runs north from
here to the Midlands, where it joins the
Grand Union and Coventry Canals to
form an important link in the
canal network. The Oxford
Canal company obtained its
Act in April 1769 and
appointed James Brindley as the
engineer. However, although Brindley
was perhaps the most renowned of all
the canal engineers, his time with the
Oxford was rather unsucessful and
relations between the company and himself were always strained, particularly
after it was found that instead of the
canal meeting the Coventry Canal on the
level, the Oxford was almost 7in (17cm)
too high, a heinous crime! Brindley died
in 1772, with the canal construction
running late and over budget. It reached
Banbury in 1778 where the company
stopped for some years to lick its
wounds. It was not until 1786, after the
company had gone back to Parliament
for a further Act, that more money could
be raised and the remainder of the route
to Oxford determined. Thereafter, the 27
miles (44km) to Oxford were constructed
without further difficulty and it was on
New Year's Day, 1790, a few months

N

A40(T)

① King's Lock

after the Thames and Severn Canal had opened, that the Oxford Canal was complete, and so Oxford was linked almost at the same time to both the Midlands and the West. The canal enabled coal from the Midlands to travel directly to Oxford and beyond, and the church bells could ring out joyously for '... rejoicing at ye coals coming to Oxford on ye New Canal...'. At Wolvercote is the site of the original papermill for Oxford University Press, set up by Dr John Fell, Bishop of Oxford in the 17th century.

ROUTE DIRECTIONS

1. Follow the meandering river to King's Lock, crossing over a footbridge across a weir on the Wytham Stream by Hagley Pool. Continue along the towpath under the Oxford bypass.

Eynsham, famous at one time for its great abbey – now long gone

ALL THAT REMAINS of Godstow Nunnery are a few fragmentary stone walls. Yet this was an aristocratic foundation, its most famous resident being the beautiful Rosamund Clifford, who died in 1176.

The Trout Inn, which stands at one end of Godstow Bridge, was clearly associated with the nunnery. Tradition suggests that it was the guest house and if this is so, then the Trout has been catering for walkers for over 800 years. Godstow Lock and the bridge over the lock cut were built in 1788 and in digging the cut the workmen disturbed the tombs of the prioresses of Godstow. In among the watermeadows runs the raised causeway from the Thames to Binsey church. St Margaret's Well, in the churchyard, has traditionally been a place of pilgrimage for those seeking a cure for ailments of the eye. The Perch Inn at Binsey is said to be haunted by the ghost of a sailor.

ROUTE DIRECTIONS

1. Cross the plank bridge over a stream and continue to Godstow Bridge, where the Trout Inn stands on the other side of the river. Carry on past the ruined wall of Godstow Nunnery to Godstow Lock.
2. Pass by Godstow Lock (the vast unenclosed Port Meadow is on your left across the river) and continue along the towpath crossing a footbridge. The footpath and causeway to Binsey turns off to your right.
3. Follow the towpath to Medley.

Godstow Bridge and the Trout inn

WOLVERCOTE

①

GODSTOW

②

③

BINSEY

A34(T)

BINSEY

MEDLEY

① ②

OSNEY

A420

③

④

⑤

⑥

Oxford (Osney Bridge) to Abingdon

9½ miles (15km)

This reach of the river, although it passes close to the centre of Oxford, is surprisingly rural in aspect; cattle still step down into the river. We start at Osney, site of the great abbey, and end at Abingdon, where stood another great abbey.

ROUTE DIRECTIONS

1. Turn left at Bossom's Boatyard, taking the footbridge over the main stream of the Thames where there used to be a weir.

2. Once across the main stream turn right to follow the towpath, with the river on your right and Bossom's private moorings in the old weir stream on your left. Cross another footbridge.

3. Carry on along the towpath and turn right to cross the footbridge over the mill stream with the railway on your left (on the site of Osney Abbey). Follow the gravel towpath which runs below houses and gardens to emerge at Osney Bridge on to the A40.

4. Turn right and cross Osney Bridge. Turn left back on to the towpath, crossing the bridge over the mill stream. Follow the towpath where it joins East Street.

5. Pass the terraced cottages and the Waterman's Arms to arrive at Osney Lock. Cross two small weir bridges and then a longer girder bridge over the weir stream and bear left along the towpath, passing the obelisk commemorating Edgar George Wilson who drowned here in heroic circumstances in 1889.

6. Follow the towpath under the main line railway bridge and round a meander loop. On your right is Grandpont Nature Park, landscaped on the site of Oxford Gas Works, which closed in 1960.

7. Continue along the towpath past a college residence and a row of cottages to Folly Bridge. Climb to the road and back down again on to the towpath.

OXFORD

OXFORD

OXFORD, THE TOWN on the old 'oxen-ford' across the river, was built in a fine defensive position on a tongue of dry land between the Thames and its tributary, the Cherwell. It is first mentioned in the Anglo Saxon Chronicle of, but had probably been in existence for about 200 years previously. By 1071 a castle had been built here by the Normans, of which St George's Tower remains. It was from Oxford Castle, besieged by King Stephen in 1142, that Matilda escaped in a snowstorm and fled across the frozen Thames to Wallingford. Since the 13th century Oxford has been a university town, and it is as such that it is known worldwide today.

The city centre can be reached from Folly Bridge via St Aldgate's, where there is a Tourist Information Centre. Oxford is particularly rich in history and in superb architecture, with 653 buildings designated as being of 'architectural or historical merit'. Chief among these are the university buildings. It is not possible here to do Oxford justice, and selection has been inevitable. The colleges, 39 in all, are dotted about and range in age from 13th-century to the present day. Most are at least partly open to the public, but their opening times vary. Proceeding along St

Christ Church's Tom Quad and Tom Tower (left), Grandpont, south of Christ Church (bottom left), The Radcliffe Camera, surrounded by college buildings (above)

Aldgate's we reach spacious Christ Church College built in 1546 by Cardinal Wolsey (as Cardinal College) and then by Henry VIII, from the spoils of nearby Osney Abbey. Here is Oxford's largest quad, Tom Quad, and Tom Tower – the lower half built by Wolsey, the upper by Sir Christopher Wren – which houses Great Tom, a 6-ton bell, from Osney. Christ Church's vaulted 800-year-old chapel is also Oxford Cathedral, and has been since the time of Henry VIII. It was originally part of the Priory of St Frideswide. There is a fine picture gallery displaying Christ Church's superb private collection of mainly Italian 14th-to 18th-century art, while the wide green and the tree-lined paths of Christ Church Meadow lie between the college and the Rivers Thames and Cherwell.

Cornmarket, the road straight across, is Oxford's main shopping street, while High Street is lined with ancient colleges and the University Church of St Mary, from whose tower there is a superb panoramic view of the city. St Edmund Hall is the oldest (1220) and one of the smallest of the colleges, while Magdalen (1459) is one of the largest. From the tower at 6am on May Morning (1 May) a springtime carol is sung in an ancient ceremony, after which Morris dancers weave their way through the streets. At Magdalen Bridge punts are for hire.

The Radcliffe Camera, which has the third largest dome in Britain, stands opposite the university church in Radcliffe Square. Dating from 1739, the building houses part of the Bodleian Library, an important collection of over two million volumes begun 300 years ago. North of Radcliffe Square, up Catte

Street, is Broad Street, a road of shops (including the bookshop, Blackwells) and more colleges. Here, in a converted warehouse, Oxford's history is told through sights, sounds and smells; it is called The Oxford Story. The Sheldonian Theatre was the first building designed by Sir Christopher Wren, and he built it for Gilbert Sheldon, Archbishop of Canterbury, to prevent the university church being used as a playhouse. Wren designed it to resemble a Roman amphitheatre, in that it is semicircular, and decorated it with pillars and balconies. It is used for graduation ceremonies. The stone heads of 18 Roman emperors on the pillars outside were sculpted in the 1970s to replace the originals, which had eroded so much as to be unrecognisable.

At the junction of Broad Street and St Giles, said to be the widest street in Europe, stands Balliol College (1263), its wooden door still scorched from the fires of 1555 and 1556 when first Bishops Latimer and Ridley and then Archbishop Cranmer were burned alive, publicly, for their Protestant faith. A small cross in the road marks the actual spot. Lower down St Giles is the Martyrs Memorial, erected in their memory. Nearby is the Eagle and Child pub, where Tolkein used to meet his friends. There is a fair in the middle of St Giles on the Monday after the first Sunday in September.

The Ashmolean Museum in Beaumont Street, off St Giles to the west, is the oldest public museum in Britain. It opened in 1683 and is most rewarding to visit, especially for its archaeological exhibits which include most of the material recovered from the upper Thames.

GRANDPONT

NEW
HINKSEY

IFFLEY

A423(T)

① ②

PASSING BY HINKSEY we can reflect that Turner stood on the hill which rises to the west to paint his pictures of Oxford's 'dreaming spires'. Ruskin was here too, and made a sketch of the little church by the stream. Around the church there's still a village feel, and yet how all has changed, for Hinksey was truly rural in those days. Yet, in 1861, Matthew Arnold began 'Thyrsis', the sequel to his tale of the 'Scholar Gipsy', with the complaint: 'How changed is here each spot man makes or fills! At the two Hinkseys nothing keeps the same.'

Iffley, down beside the Thames a little way above Kennington Island, is an idyllic poplar-shaded spot, with attractive balustraded footbridges and a magnificent Norman church on the hill above. Today the suburbia of Oxford crowds in closely, but at Iffley you are hardly aware of that; it possesses a rural charm. This place has been visited and loved by generations of Oxford undergraduates, and is traditionally full of student digs. During the last war the poet Keith Douglas, who was killed in Normandy when only 24, wrote a poem in which, knowing that he might die, he wondered what cataclysm could possibly prevent his shade from returning to the punt gliding towards Iffley. The Norman church was built on a massive scale in 1170-80, being the gift of a rich patron. It is known that the St Remy family held Iffley in the second half of the 12th century, and it is thought that it was probably built by Robert de St Remy and given by his daughter, Juliana, to Kenilworth Priory. The great doorways are carved with animals, birds and fishes, and the solid square tower rises grandly in three stages; within, the Norman nave speaks of strength, the 12th-century font is of black marble and there is plenty of 15th-century glass.

Iffley Lock, alongside the lovely lock island beneath the poplar trees, was one of the first on the Thames. Replaced many times, the present structure dates from 1924. An old lock is used as a weir. On one side of the island are the boat rollers and on the other a bridge takes you over the old mill stream to Iffley village. The picturesque old watermill was destroyed by fire long ago, in 1908, but part of it was rebuilt as Grist Cottage.

This reach of the river is famous as that used in the Oxford May Eights, and Iffley is the start of the famous 'bumping races'.

ROUTE DIRECTIONS

1. Follow the towpath, with Christ Church Meadow across the river to your left, and pass the Isis Tavern. Go over two footbridges to Iffley Lock (cross the lock by the wooden footbridge to visit the village and Norman church).
2. Carry on with the river on your left and cross the wide Hinksey stream by the wooden footbridge. Continue under the A423(T).

New Hinksey Weir on the Cherwell before it merges with the Thames

Sandford Lock, the deepest on the river above Teddington

THOMAS DE SAUNFORD gave the manor of Sandford to the Knights Templar in 1240, and they set up a preceptory here. This brotherhood of the 'poor soldiers of the Temple of Solomon' was formed to protect pilgrims on their journey to the Holy Land. The preceptory flourished, but in 1308 the Order was savagely suppressed. Sandford's Preceptor, William Sautre, was imprisoned at Aldgate, where he died. Today the name Temple Farm gives a clue to the past. The farmhouse itself dates from the 16th century, but the old barn near by, with three blocked lancet windows and a 15th-century doorway, was the Templar's chapel.

Early on in the reign of Elizabeth I, the Napiers were lords of the manor at Sandford. George Napier, a Jesuit, was captured in 1568 and executed in Oxford. His quartered body was displayed on the four gates of the city and his head on the front of Christ Church. By night his grieving relatives collected the dismembered body – apart from the head, which, being inside the city, was beyond their reach – and gave him a decent burial. So much for the facts. But here we have another Thames-side ghost, for it is said that every Christmas Eve George Napier drives a ghostly coach and four from Temple Farm to Oxford, searching for his head. Anyone who meets him will die within the year.

The porch of St Andrew's Church at Sandford was rebuilt in 1652 by Dame Eliza Isham, and her name appears along with the date and the words POR-TICUS PATRONAE (patron of the porch), with the rhyming couplet:

'Thankes to thy Charitie religiose Dame Which found mee olde and made mee new again'.

Sandford Pool is deep and dangerous. Over the years five Christ Church under-graduates have drowned there, and the obelisk by the weir commemorates them. It is hidden behind trees and railings from the Thames Path. It seems strange that all the fatalities have been from Christ Church. One of them was Michael Llewelyn Davies, the Michael of J. M. Barrie's *Peter Pan*.

Sandford Lock is the deepest lock on the Thames, with a fall of 8ft 10in (2.7m). Along with Iffley, it was one of the origi-nal Thames locks. Sandford Mill, first built in 1294, was followed by many a working successor. The most recent mill on the site was first used for grinding corn, but was later converted for the manufacture of coloured paper. Until recently the tall mill chimney dominated the scene, but that has been replaced by smart riverside housing.

ROUTE DIRECTIONS

1. Go under the railway bridge and keep on going where a path cuts off a meander loop and turn left over a footbridge spanning Sandford's millstream intake.
2. Continue with the main river still on your left and cross three footbridges where the weir streams flow into deep Sandford Pool (after the first footbridge notice the sad old wrecks on the opposite bank). Continue to Sandford Lock and continue on past the lock cottage (cross the lock to reach the King's Head).
3. Cross the concrete bridge where the old mill stream rejoins the Thames and keep going along the towpath.

KENNINGTON

SANDFORD

A4200

① ② ③ P

LOWER
BRADLEY

RADLEY IS KNOWN for its public school, founded in 1847 by Dr Sewell. Radley Hall, the Queen Anne mansion which forms the main school, is a striking building. It was the subject of a painting undertaken by Turner when he was only 14. The landscape of this stretch of the river is full of tranquil beauty, and Radley has an extremely strong rowing tradition.

Radley College is in Upper Radley, as is the 15th-century church in which is preserved, as the pulpit canopy, the late perpendicular canopy of the Speaker's Chair from the House of Commons. It came here in 1653 and was presented to Radley by Mr Speaker Lenthall, the man to whom Charles I had remarked that the birds had flown.

Lower Radley, which, as the name suggests, is nearer to the river, is the smaller village – no more than a hamlet of cottages, some thatched.

Along the banks of the Thames there were a phenomenal number of religious houses; enormous abbeys, small secluded priories, monasteries and nunneries. The priories of Cricklade and Lechlade, for example, the nunneries at Godstow and Goring, and the abbeys of Dorchester, Reading, Medmenham, Bisham, Eynsham, Abingdon, Osney, Chertsey and Westminster. Now all the abbeys, with the exception of Westminster, have vanished. Some, like Osney, have gone so utterly that there is no trace that they were ever there. Yet these were the institutions that founded the wealth of the Thames; the monks drained the riverside marshes, made use of the rich meadows and harnessed the power of the river for mills to grind their corn. During the Middle Ages, as Hilaire Belloc pointed out in his *Historic Thames*, the overwhelming impression received by a bargeman going down the Thames would have been the splendour of the abbeys.

First, there was Eynsham, a great Benedictine foundation. Aelfric was abbot there for 20 years, translating the scriptures into English and writing the lives of the saints against a background of the repeated raids of the Danes. In this way Aelfric carried on the traditions and work of Alfred the Great, helping the English people via the new English language. The abbey was dissolved by Henry VIII and since then has been broken up for building materials.

The medieval bargeman, rounding the meander by Wytham Great Wood and passing Godstow's nunnery, ' ... would already have seen far off, larger and a little nearer than the many spires of Oxford .... the Abbey of Osney. It would have been his landmark, as Hereford is the landmark for a man today rowing up the Wye.'

Today there is nothing even to mark the site of the abbey. It was founded in the reign of Henry I and rebuilt in 1287 in such magnificence that its towers and windows were among the chief glories of Oxford. It was destroyed at the Dissolution and Wolsey used its materials and money in the building of Christ Church.

Abingdon Abbey was the next downstream from Osney. It would have come into sight at first screened from the river by trees and then, a moment later, showing the full glory of its west front. This great Benedictine abbey was founded in AD675, but was sacked repeatedly by the Danes. It was refounded in AD955 by Athelwold and began to expand and flourish, attracting tradespeople to its gates. William the Conqueror celebrated Easter there in 1084, and rode away leaving his young son in the hands of the monks, to be given a Christian education. The abbey reached the height of its prosperity in the years 1100-1117 under Abbot Fabritius, and thereafter declined, to perish utterly at the Dissolution. Below Abingdon comes Dorchester, until the Norman Conquest a cathedral city. The abbey church of St Peter and St Paul stands on the site of the original cathedral and was built after 1170 when the Augustinian abbey was founded here, replacing the earlier abbey founded in AD635. The survival of the church following the Dissolution in 1536 is due to the generosity of a rich citizen, Richard Beauforest, who bought it and bequeathed it to the parish. It is one of the most magnificent parish churches in England and contains many treasures, above all a wonderful Jesse window.

ROUTE DIRECTIONS

1. Continue with the river on your left, increasingly enclosed by high banks.
2. Cross over the footbridge by Radley's boat house and continue along the towpath.

THE COURTENAYS WERE lords of the manor at Nuneham from 1214 until 1710, when Viscount Harcourt bought the estate. In 1756 Lord Harcourt set about building a new and fashionable house in the truly Classical style. This was done in such a way that from the villa and its park the skyline of Oxford was visible (suggesting views of Rome from the Campagna), a vista that involved the destruction of old Nuneham village. This demolition of old villages was very common during the 18th century and many labourers were thus dispossessed. But Lord Harcourt was not a man to dispossess his tenants. He built an entirely new village for them on the Oxford Road away from the river and modestly out of sight of the Nuneham House. This action divided public opinion. Society and the House of Commons thought that the cottagers were very lucky to have new houses, others were not so convinced. Among the latter was the playwright and poet, Oliver Goldsmith. His long poem, 'The Deserted Village', which deplores the

depopulation of the countryside, is thought to describe the scene at Nuneham.

...The man of wealth and pride Takes up a space that many poor supplied – Space for his lake, his park's extended bounds, Space for his horses, equipage, and hounds; The robe that wraps his limbs in silken sloth, Has robbed the neighbouring fields of half their growth; His seat, where solitary sports are seen, Indignant spurns the cottage from the green ...

The 2nd Lord Harcourt employed more distinguished architects, including Robert Adam, and put the landscaping of the park into the hands of Lancelot 'Capability' Brown. The monument visible on the top of the hill is the Carfax Conduit, which once stood in the centre of Oxford. It was built in 1616 as an elaborately carved water container and contained two cisterns, one to supply water to the university and a second to supply the town. It was obsolete by the 1780s and Oxford gave it to Lord Harcourt who set it up in his grounds as an eye-catcher.

N

In 1840, Queen Victoria and Prince Albert spent part of their honeymoon at Nuneham Park. In her letters the Queen wrote that she found the view down the Thames valley 'remarkably fine'.

Locks Wood is named after Nuneham Lock that stood here, and was first mentioned in 1576, but a poundlock was never built on the site.

ROUTE DIRECTIONS

1. Continue with Nuneham House and the old Carfax conduit prominent on the opposite bank, which is verdant with dense woodland.
2. Carry on beside the river and under the railway bridge into open meadows. Bear right on to a fenced path beside the river (at this point a ferry crossed and the towpath moved to the opposite bank). Opposite is the entrance to the Swift Ditch.

Abingdon, with the open fields of Andersey Island in the foreground

Abingdon to Benson

12 miles (19.5km)

N

ROUTE DIRECTIONS

1. Follow the fenced path round the little marshy backwater and back towards the river with the Abbey Stream on your right. Turn right over the footbridge and right again to continue along the path with the Abbey Stream now on your left. Visible beyond is Abingdon Lock on the Thames itself.

2. Cross the stile and turn left to take the wooden footbridge, signed to Abbey Meadow, over the Abbey Stream. Turn left again towards Abingdon Lock and follow the path across the weir and towards the lower lock gates (note the stone from the old weir set in the concrete of the new and reading 'This lock was built by George Stonehouse and Richard Adams Anno 1649').

3. Go through the gate and turn right to rejoin the towpath. Continue along the towpath to Abingdon Bridge with the spire of St Helen's visible ahead.

4. From Abingdon Bridge continue along the towpath with the river and Abingdon on your right. To your left is the old causeway across Andersey Island (the land between the Thames and the Swift Ditch), with the modern road alongside it.

5. Pass, on the opposite bank, the entrance to a marina and then cross the Swift Ditch by the wooden footbridge (the old stone Culham Bridge is near by to your left).

6. Keep going along the towpath with large fields and the village of Culham on your left and Didcot power station ahead.

This section of the walk follows the Thames towpath through delightful scenery under the lee of the Sinodun Hills, past the ancient town of Dorchester. Abingdon, with its open river frontage, beautiful old bridge, magnificent town hall and quaint rows of almshouses, all crowned by the soaring spire of St Helen's Church, is regarded by many as the most beautiful town on the Thames. It grew up in front of the great abbey which extended along the Thames to the north-east, although Domesday mentions only 'ten traders before the gates'. Formerly, Abingdon was the county town of Berkshire, but the 1974 county boundary changes moved it into Oxfordshire.

ABINGDON DEVELOPED in the shadow of its great abbey, and today the grand old gatehouse surveys the market place knowingly, as if to remind the town of the original cause of its 900 years of prosperity. Apart from this gatehouse and a couple of other old buildings, the abbey is a memory which lurks down by the river in Abbey Meadows.

Abingdon prospered exceedingly during the Middle Ages and its burghers waxed fat on the spoils of their woollen trade. This led to bitter wrangles between the abbey and the town. The Abingdon merchants formed themselves into the Guild or fraternity of the Holy Cross and set about improving their town. They built Abingdon Bridge, the

causeway across Andersey Island which now runs alongside the main road and Culham Bridge across the Swift Ditch, on land obtained from the Abbot of Abingdon by Royal Charter in 1416. The Guild also built the almshouses and the splendid Church of St Helen.

St Helen's is a spacious building, mostly a 15th- and 16th-century remodelling of a 13th-century church. The eye-catching spire rises graciously for 150ft (45.5m). Within, the roof paintings of the north aisle have been dated to about 1390 and, as an ensemble, are unique. In the market place in central Abingdon, where the great Monday Market still flourishes as it has since before 1086, stands the magnificent market hall.

ROUTE DIRECTIONS

1. Follow the towpath round to the left beside Culham Cut.

2. Turn right to take the footbridge over the cut and bear right with a wire fence on your right to the footbridges over the weirs of Sutton Pool. Cross a channel of the Thames and turn right over another footbridge. Carry on over three more footbridges – the last is where Sutton Mill used to stand. Walk up a gravel drive to the road.

3. Turn left along Appleford Road and then left again opposite the Fish pub over a stile signed 'Thames Path ½ mile'. Go down a concrete drive to a stile. Cross the stile and follow the path with the Thames on your left till you reach the road and the cottages at Sutton Bridge. Turn left along the road to cross Sutton Bridge and continue across the bridge by the lock at Culham Cut. Turn right over a stile back on to the towpath.

4. Carry on along the towpath and under the electricity transmission lines.

CULHAM IS A LOVELY village, basking peacefully around its green. Many of its houses are spacious and dignified, including the Old Vicarage and Culham House. The manor house is mainly Jacobean, having been rebuilt in the early 1600s, but includes part of the medieval grange of the Abbots of Abingdon. In the grounds is a dovecote of 1685. Culham Lock and Cut were excavated in 1809 to bypass Sutton Mill, the weirs and the weir pools which slowed down the passage of barge traffic. The weirs at Sutton Pools have been modernised, but there is still an excitement at the rushing

water and the nearby tranquillity of the tree-lined pools. Single-arched Sutton Bridge was built in 1807 to replace Sutton Ferry. In 1793 Widow Hewit was in charge of the ferry, and in 1798 Daniel Gibbons was the ferryman, paid 24 shillings a month.

Sutton was already a village of some 30 dwellings when it was given to the abbots of Abingdon in AD687. They built a grange here and a 14th-century house south of the church is still known as The Abbey. Reginald Courtenay received the manor from William the Conqueror, and the village became Sutton Courtenay.

Norman Hall, which stands near the church, is indeed a Norman manor house of 1190-1200. There is also a Tudor manor house.

The village repays exploration, for here, running happily along the road and backing on to the Thames, are old gabled houses in attractive groups. George Orwell (Eric Blair) and Herbert Asquith, who was the last Liberal prime minister (1908-16), are buried in the churchyard. Asquith spent his retirement at Sutton Courtenay in a gabled house called The Wharf, a name redolent of Sutton's past as a river port.

B4016

①

APPLEFORD

APPLEFORD CHURCH SPIRE can be seen across the river. Somewhere in the churchyard beside the church of St Peter and St Paul, in an unmarked grave, lies John Faulkner, a famous jockey who rode his last race at the amazing age of 74! That was at Abingdon in 1902; but old John lived for another 33 years, dying on the eve of his 105th birthday. His way of life obviously suited him, for he was father of 32 children. Clifton Cut was opened in 1822, and bypasses Long Wittenham where Robert Gibbings, author of two books on the River Thames, *Sweet Thames Run Softly* and *Till I end My Song*, lived in his retirement.

Wittenham Clumps, the rings of trees that crown the Sinodun Hills brood over the Thames valley. One of the hills, Castle Hill, is crowned by the ramparts of a large Iron Age camp – the most important strategic site of this age in southern England.

ROUTE DIRECTIONS

1. Go under the main railway line,with the church spire at Appleford visible on the opposite bank. Continue over a footbridge to Clifton Cut.

2. Pass the weir where the natural meander of the Thames bears right to Long Wittenham.

CLIFTON
HAMPDEN

A415

②

P

B4015

①

LONG
WITTENHAM

CLIFTON HAMPDEN BRIDGE, a red-brick structure of seven arches, looks much older than it is. It was built in 1857, with bricks specially made at Clifton Hampden, to a design by Sir George Gilbert Scott. Across the bridge is the thatched old pub, the Barley Mow, parts of which date from 1350. It was partially destroyed by fire in 1975, but has been well restored.

Clifton Hampden clings to the steep river cliff on the left-hand bank of the Thames beyond the bridge. It is a cosy village of quaint brick-and-timber thatched cottages and colourful gardens sloping to the Thames. The little Church of St Michael and All Angels, restored by Scott, is reached up a flight of steep stone stairs. In Clifton Hampden churchyard rests Sergeant William Dykes who accidently fired the first shot at Waterloo, and so precipitated the battle.

ROUTE DIRECTIONS

1. Go alongside the narrow artificial channel and through the gates at Clifton Lock where the cut rejoins the river. Continue along the towpath to Clifton Hampden.
2. Climb up on to Clifton Hampden Bridge and turn right. Turn left to continue along the towpath with the Thames now on your left.

Dorchester, a few miles downstream

① ② ③

LITTLE
WITTENHAM

P

DORCHESTER WAS ONCE an important cathedral city and it contains one of the earliest Christian shrines; yet today it is totally bypassed by the main road and its venerable history obscured by picturesque cottages. For nearly 500 years it was an important see of the West Saxons and then of the Mercians, but the see was moved to Lincoln shortly after the Norman Conquest.

Dorchester in fact pre-dates the Saxons; it is circled by defensive works of the Iron Age. The Romans were here too, building a camp and then a garrison town, and parts of their town walls still stand. In the 7th century the bishopric was established and the town flourished. Dorchester is forever connected with the life of St Birinus, who founded the first abbey here in 635. Birinus baptised Cyneglis, King of the West Saxons, here at Dorchester, with the saintly Oswald of Northumbria acting as sponsor. This baptism would have taken place in the river – whether the Thame or the Thames is impossible to say – for total immersion was the normal way of entering the Christian Faith at that time.

The 'Dyke Hills', down in the meadow near the Thames, are part of the Iron Age defence system dating from the earliest phase of Dorchester's history. These double banks were constructed to make secure a defensive site by fortifying the north sides of a peninsula of land between the rivers Thames and Thame, which is bounded by the rivers on the west and south and east. In times of danger the tribe and its livestock would find safety in this 114-acre (46ha) enclosure. The main gauging station for the measurement of flow of the upper Thames is situated at Day's Lock.

The River Thame flows into the Thames opposite Little Wittenham Wood. Downstream from here the united waters of these rivers are known by all as the Thames, and the name Isis is left behind.

ROUTE DIRECTIONS

1. Walk round the great meander bend to Day's Lock. On your left are the Iron Age ramparts known as the Dyke Hills and the ancient town of Dorchester-on-Thames.
2. Turn left and cross the weir and river at Day's Lock. Then turn right along the towpath.
3. Continue along the towpath with the river on your right and beyond it the steep wooded slope of Little Wittenham Wood (a nature reserve) and the grassy Sinodun Hills, crowned by the Wittenham Clumps.

4. Cross the steel footbridge over the river Thames at its confluence with the Thames and continue round the next meander bend.

A423(T)

② ①

SHILLINGFORD

OLD STREET FORD is the point where the Roman road from Silchester, near Reading, crossed the Thames on its way to Alchester, near Bicester.

Shillingford is a pleasant village, with a village street that leads down to the willow-lined Thames at a former wharf which served a brewery. Indeed, Shillingford is well supplied with hostelries: from the well-known Shillingford Bridge Hotel on the far bank of the river, to the Bell and the Kingfisher on the old Oxford-to-Henley coaching route, now the A423(T).

Shillingford Bridge was built in 1827

Looking back over Dorchester to Berinsfield

N

ROUTE DIRECTIONS

1. Turn left away from the river and go up the field to a stile on the A423.

2. Cross the stile and turn right along the road into Shillingford. Turn right at the Kingfisher pub. Just before you reach the river turn left along an alley beside the flood marks. Bear right along another alley past the gates of Shillingford Court. Continue through the gate into the lane and turn left. Walk along the lane to emerge at the road opposite the former ferry house. Turn right to Shillingford Bridge.

3. Do not cross the bridge but turn left along the towpath beneath a row of poplars.

③

A329

as part of a turnpike venture with Reading as its destination. It is a graceful bridge of three lovely arches which form great semi circles above the river. The bridge was partly rebuilt in 1906.

About 2 miles (3.4km) upstream from Shillingford Bridge there used to be a ferry known as Keen Edge. This is thought to be a corruption of 'Cane Hedge', a description of the osier banks of the Thames. Osiers – willows grown to produce canes for fish traps, basket-making and other wicker-work articles – were a common crop along the Thames where the rich alluvial soil was excellent for their production. Sets of two years' growth are planted, which were ready for cropping in about three years and which continued in production for about 15 years.

A423(T)

BENSON

① ② ③ ④

Benson to Pangbourne

11¼ miles (18km)

This stretch of the river includes the famous Goring Gap between Goring and Whitchurch. Here the Thames enters the only hilly section of its course, in the lovely valley between the Berkshire Downs and the Chilterns cut by the river during the Ice Age. The landscape is pleasing, wooded and full of variety. Walking is easy, though variable: chalk, grass, earth, gravel and asphalt.

BENSON SHOULD PROPERLY be known as Bensington, though these days the shorter variant is generally preferred. In Saxon times it was the capital of the Gevissae tribe. A century later Offa, King of Mercia, won a great victory here beating back the West Saxons. Yet there is little of antiquity here today down in the meadows beside the Thames, apart from the 13th-century church.

During the coaching era Benson was a famous coaching post, and its inns still testify to its history. During those days coach building was the main employment of the village. Today it is shadowed by its RAF base.

Benson Lock occupies the site of an ancient weir and watermill, the latter mentioned in 1396 as the property of local landowner John James and his wife, Christiana. There is a reference to the weir in a manuscript of 1585, stating the names of owners and weirkeepers, while the existence of a flashlock is confirmed in 1746. The first poundlock here was built in 1788. It is intriguing to learn that 'some Low Country Men' were employed in the construction of Benson Lock. Thacker wondered: 'Were they Dutchmen, who would perhaps be natural adepts at this kind of work? The fact that they were paid 2s 2d per day, while ordinary labourers received only 1s 4d – 1s 9d, may seem evidence in favour of the conjecture...'.

ROUTE DIRECTIONS

1. Pass a caravan park on the edge of Benson.
2. Where the towpath ends, head obliquely up a small public garden to a waymarked gap into Benson. Turn right along the lane.
3. Go down the lane and then turn right through the gate beside the small car park and cross the footbridge to Benson Lock.
4. Cross the lower lock gates and turn left to follow the towpath into Wallingford.

Benson Lock and Weir. The village has some attractive old inns

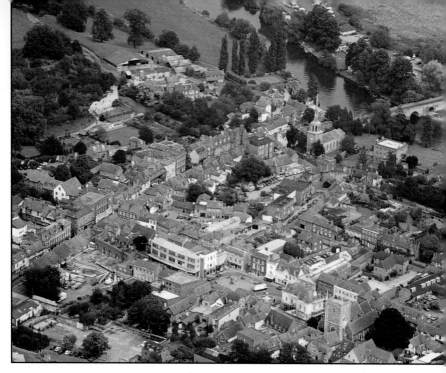

From the river, Wallingford is dominated by the distinctive spire of St Peter's Church

ROUTE DIRECTIONS

1. Cross the road and go down Thames Street with St Peter's Church on the left. Carry on past the entrance to Castle Priory.
2. At St Leonard's Lane turn left to follow a path round the edge of the churchyard, over a stream and through an arch in the centre of a terrace of cottages (note flood mark; Nov 1894).
3. Bear left into Wharf Lane with the tall chimneys of an old house to your right. Continue along the lane which becomes an enclosed path.
4. Go across the boatyard to rejoin the towpath. Keep going and cross a footbridge over a ditch.
5. Carry on into the open to follow the path along the grassy bank (the Ridgeway National Trail is running parallel to the Thames Path here, but on the opposite side of the river).

WALLINGFORD IS AN attractive and friendly old market town with a good selection of pubs and shops. It was founded by the Romans who built a fortress here overlooking the river at a point where it could be forded and later developed as a Saxon burgh, although it is not known to which age the town owes its 'grid iron' street pattern. It suffered the common fate of being sacked by the Danes. William the Conqueror came to Wallingford in 1066 on his circuitous route to London, and instructed Robert D'Oyley to build both a castle and a bridge. To this Norman castle came the Norman monarchs and their retinues. Empress Matilda took refuge here during the Civil War between herself and King Stephen in 1142, and Henry II, Matilda's son, came here too when he had concluded the treaty with Stephen which secured him the succession, and who gave Wallingford its first charter in 1155. King John came here; the Black Prince came here and so did his wife Joan, the fair Maid of Kent, who was trying desperately to patch up the quarrel between her son, Richard II, and his uncle, John of Gaunt.

Today little of the castle remains; it lies to the right of the Thames towpath before Wallingford Bridge. The antiquary William Camden (1551-1623) said of it, 'its size and magnificence used to strike me with amazement, when I came thither a lad from Oxford; it being a retreat for students of the church'. Wallingford Bridge is in part medieval, although much of it was rebuilt in 1809 when it was widened. Its 17 arches date from that time, the length of the bridge being an attempt to keep the roadway above flood level.

The oldest extant church in Wallingford is St Leonard's which retains some Norman features, notably the richly carved arches opening into the chancel and the apse. Now redundant, St Peter's is the proud possessor of an eye-catching spire which rises from an octagonal lantern. The church was ruined during the Civil war and was rebuilt during the 18th century. St Mary's Church, near the town hall, has been heavily restored.

WALLINGFORD

P

① ② ③ ④ ⑤

A329

The church at Cholsey stands well away from the village to the north-west

MONGEWELL PARK, now Carmel College, a Jewish public school, has a 3-mile (4.8km) long frontage on the opposite side of the Thames.

North Stoke stands in a delightful stretch of the Thames valley, on the opposite side of the river to the Thames Path where woods crowd down the valley sides towards the water. It is thought that the church here, whose square tower rises against a backdrop of trees, was probably founded by St Birinus. It is dedicated to St Mary of Bec, since monks from the great abbey at Bec in Normandy were invited to settle here in the years after the Norman Conquest. Today's church, however, was built between 1240 and 1300.

The famous Edwardian contralto, Dame Clara Butt, lived at Brook Lodge, North Stoke, for many years until her death in 1936. Elgar wrote his 'Sea Pictures' for her, though it was her records of sentimental ballads that brought her fame and fortune.

Cholsey Marsh Nature Reserve, on the same side of the river as the Thames Path, is run by BBONT (pronounced Bee-Bont), the Berkshire, Buckinghamshire and Oxfordshire Naturalists' Trust. This wild area of damp watermeadows alongside the river near the site of the former Little Stoke ferry is managed by traditional methods so that it contains a host of wild flowers and is a haven for small birds and mammals. Up till the middle of the last century laden corn wagons were ferried across here. Little Stoke, on the far side of the river, is no more

NORTH STOKE

①

② ★

LITTLE STOKE

than a fistful of houses, one of them the former ferryman's cottage. In 1787 the ferryman was a William Brown. The lane followed up to the Fair Mile Hospital is part of the 'Papist Way', a road which ran from Cholsey Abbey to the river at Little Stoke ferry. The monastery at Cholsey only existed for 20 years (AD986-1006), after which it was utterly destroyed by the Danes.

ROUTE DIRECTIONS

N

1. Continue past North Stoke on the opposite side of the river to reach Cholsey Marsh Nature Reserve, run by BBONT. Turn right away from the Thames up the lane (this was the site of the Little Stoke ferry).
2. Continue up the lane, past the Fair Mile Hospital on your right, to the A329.
3. Turn left along the main road and continue over the railway bridge.

MOULSFORD

①

②

A329

THE BRUNEL RAILWAY bridge of 1839 is just a little way down the path beyond the turn-off for Moulsford. It is something of a masterpiece as it crosses the river obliquely and the brick courses are twisted, giving a weird effect when looked at from below. The bridge was widened in 1892 by building a separate bridge alongside, some 6ft (2m) away from the original structure.

Moulsford is a village of red-brick old cottages. Down beside the river under the shade of a weeping willow is the small 14th-century church of St John the Baptist, with its shingled spire and a bell turret. This was restored in 1846 by Sir G. G. Scott for the princely sum of £64. South Stoke, on the opposite side of the river, has an Early English church, dedicated to St Andrew, with an embattled tower and belfry. The church contains a memorial to a South Stoke man, Griffith Higgs, who died in 1659. Brought up on a farm here, he rose to be Dean of Lichfield and chaplain to Princess Elizabeth, the sister of Charles I. She married the Elector Palatine and later became the Queen of Bohemia, the very lady to whom Sir Henry Wotton addressed his immortal poem: 'You meaner beauties of the night...'.

Elizabeth of Bohemia's grandson was George I, the king who spoke no English and, on account of this, left Parliament to its own devices and was responsible for raising Walpole to the position of prime minister.

Moulsford ferry ran from the Beetle and Wedge pub, down by the Thames, over to South Stoke, charging sixpence a (one way) journey. If business was slack in the bar the ferryman-cum-barman would row you across at any time, if not you had to fit in with the timetabled three crossings a day. A bell was used to summon the ferry. In January 1673 there was a terrible flood at South Stoke, when the river burst its banks and '... a Boat was rowed over the Tops of the Moore Hedges down to the Vicarage gate so that most part of the Housen and Barnes of this Towne were Drowned ...'.

The Beetle and Wedge pub takes its name from the tools used in wood splitting: a beetle being a heavy mallet which is used to drive a wedge into a log. This inn has literary associations, for Bernard Shaw often visited the place and H. G. Wells stayed here while he wrote *The History of Mr Polly*. Indeed, the Beetle and Wedge was the model for the Potwell Inn.

Near the Olde Leathern Bottel, a popular riverside pub on the towpath below the Beetle and Wedge, is an old brick well, the outfall of the Cleeve Spring. This water was considered to possess curative properties for many ailments, including 'Mange, Murrians, Meazles, Melancholy dumps ...' – truly a panacea for all ills!

ROUTE DIRECTIONS

1. Carry on through Moulsford.
2. Turn left at Offlands Farm along Ferry Lane to the Beetle and Wedge pub. Go into the car park and turn right through a gate to rejoin the towpath with the Thames on your left.

The Beetle and Wedge hotel at Moulsford

Streatley stands where the Icknield Way crosses the river

ROUTE DIRECTIONS

1. Carry on along the towpath through grassy meadows and over the steep bridge of the marina entry. Continue into the meadow above Cleeve Lock.

2. Go through the gate and bear left over the little meadow and cross the footbridge on to a pathway. Go through another gate and follow the path which curves round to the left.

3. Follow the path as it joins a lane passing a white house on the right and a church on the left.

4. Turn left to reach the road in Streatley. Turn left passing the Swan Diplomat Hotel to reach Goring Bridge.

5. Cross Goring Bridge and turn right by the mill buildings to get down to the towpath again. Continue along the towpath, with the river on your right, into the Goring Gap.

STREATLEY'S CHURCH of St Mary was rebuilt in 1865 and near by is a range of malthouses that were converted into a village hall in 1898. The Swan Diplomat, down by the river, is a much modernised old inn.

Goring is Streatley's twin village. It sits on the opposite bank of the Thames and the two are joined by a bridge built in 1923 to replace the old timber bridge of 1837. The new bridge is a concrete replica of the old, and fits well into the surroundings. At one time there was a nunnery at Goring and its chapel remains as Goring's church.

A329

STREATLEY

GORING

FOURTEENTH-CENTURY Basildon church sits amid its beech trees over the river. Jethro Tull, the pioneer in mechanised agriculture, is buried in the churchyard. He was a local man of whom great things were prophesied. Called to the bar in 1699, at the age of 25, he aimed for Parliament, but ill health forced him to retire to his Basildon estates. He worked on improving the efficiency of agriculture and invented the seed drill. He died in 1741.

Until recently Gatehampton (Basildon) ferry used to ply the Thames from a point near Ferry Cottage, which is now a private house. The Thames Commissioners contemplated instigating a ferry here in 1787, but there is no further information relating to it till 1810, when Charles Emmett was employed as ferryman. Gatehampton (Basildon) railway bridge is the second of Brunel's brick bridges over the Thames downstream from Wallingford. Its construction in 1840 is said to have altered the flow of the river so as to '... spoil the best gudgeon-swim in the neighbourhood...'.

Fishing has always been a popular Thames sport, and all along the towpath the walker is in close companionship with the fisherman. Izaak Walton's *Compleat Angler* was written partly on the Thames, as the inn of that name at Marlow goes to show. These days most Thames fishing is controlled by clubs and associations so that very little free fishing is available. However, tickets (day/week/fortnight) to fish some reaches can be obtained from local tackle shops. It is possible just to watch fish from the towpath. The most numerous are gudgeon, bleak, minnow and roach. Gudgeon prefer clear water and a gravel bed and gather in large shoals in late summer. Roach and bream are also fond of gravelly reaches but the angler generally returns these fish to the river as they are not good to eat, although they provide a challenge as they have become wily in the well-fished Thames. Bream are still numerous in some reaches. These large slow-moving fish, which can live to be 50 years old, enjoy weirpools.

Above Oxford there are large

GATEHAMPTON

③

②

①

LOWER
BASILDON

numbers of barbel, a fish which is not common in other British rivers apart from the Trent. These powerful fish inhabit weirpools and reaches with strong currents. They are for the specialist angler, however, as it is not unknown for barbel to break both line and rod.

Chub are shy and hide in shoals beneath some form of cover – overhanging bushes and trees or 'rubbish rafts'. They will not venture into the open river when it is full of pleasure boats, as they dislike noise.

Pike are abundant too and all sizes are caught, including specimens in excess of 20lbs. Pike like some cover where they can lie in wait, perfectly motionless, for anything that comes their way, be it fish, waterfowl or mammal. Their powerful tail and strong jaws with ferocious teeth mean that prey rarely escapes the pike, giving it its nickname 'water wolf'.

But what about salmon, which were once so numerous in the Thames that London apprentices were fed on them, but were unknown in the river for 140 years from 1834 to 1974 due to

N

ROUTE DIRECTIONS

1. Pass under the railway bridge with Gatehampton Farm on your left. Cross the field and go through the gate and follow the path. Turn left over the footbridge with Ferry Cottage on your right (there used to be a ferry here).
2. Go up the path with a fence on your left to a bridleway on a river terrace at Gatehampton Farm.
3. Turn right along the bridleway to climb up round the meander bend and enter Lower Hartslock Wood.

pollution? Thankfully the Thames is once again clean enough to support these splendid fish but most of the weirs are too high for them to jump when they swim up-river to their natural spawning grounds so the middle Thames tributaries, such as the Loddon, the Kennet and the Pang, and the Thames Salmon Trust is involved in fitting 'fish passes' to weirs to allow the salmon an obstacle-free passage.

LOWER
BASILDON

A329

②

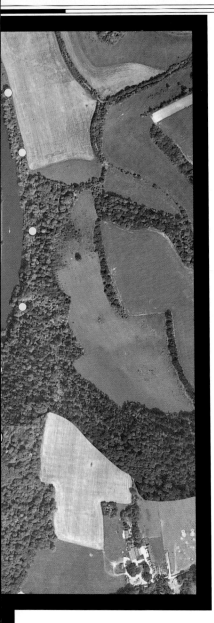

GORING GAP IS A lovely stretch of the valley of the Thames. Hartslock Wood clothes the steep eastern slopes, while on the far side of the river are low-lying open meadows backed by the steep slopes which rise to Basildon. On these low-lying meadows is the Child Beale Wildlife Trust which fronts the river and is home to a number of rare breeds of sheep, cattle and deer as well as Vietnamese pot-bellied pigs. The Beale Bird Park, with its gardens and lakes, specialises in rare and endangered birds, from owls, peacocks and parrots to cranes and ornamental pheasants. On the hillside opposite is the lovely façade of the 18th-century Basildon Park (National Trust), which is open to the public.

Hartslock Wood, which stood by the little islands under the lee of the woods, takes its name from a former lock on the river – again associated with the ubiquitous Harts. It is mentioned between 1580 and 1585 as being kept by Hugh Whysler, and then again in 1632. After this there is little evidence of its being kept in anything like a state of repair. In 1710 it was regarded as merely a 'fish lock', and by 1802 it was: 'Hart's Old Wear; the ruins of it very inconvenient'. The old timbers were ordered to be removed in 1804 and in 1812, but none of the clearance can have been very effective for in 1910 Thacker watched the final destruction of this navigational hazard. Barges were moored in the river '... still drawing the teeth of this half-extinct monster against the left bank ...'.

Beautifully landscaped grounds surround Basildon Park, another fine National Trust property within easy reach of the river

ROUTE DIRECTIONS

1. Continue along the bridleway into Hartslock Wood as it bears away to the left. Continue out of the wood on to the chalk downland and down into a little combe.
2. Pass Combe Farm on your right (the Child Beale Wildlife Trust is in the valley below).

Pangbourne to Reading Bridge

6¾ miles (10.75km)

From Whitchurch the path descends back into the Thames valley, where it follows the towpath through verdant green meadows, with only a short section of road walking in Purley and along the amazingly rural towpath into Reading.

Pangbourne – Wind in the Willows country

WHITCHURCH MAIN STREET straggles delightfully down the hillside towards the Thames and the quaint white toll bridge, built in 1880. This replaced an earlier wooden bridge of 1792, which in turn replaced a ferry. The toll was levied on all, even pedestrians, and in the 1870s local people used to walk over the weir to avoid paying it. The flashlock beneath Whitchurch was replaced by a poundlock in 1787. The fall here is large and the resultant wild water of the weir well known. Thacker was impressed, and wrote, 'This weir is indeed still a fine sight from the little ascent beside it; especially if Thames in yellow flood be mingling with the black waters of the tributary Pang'. The weir of Whitchurch Lock is known as Pangbourne Weir.

St Mary's Church was entirely rebuilt during 1858 in 14th-century style, but the Norman doorway and 15th-century porch were incorporated. Whitchurch was the birthplace of Sir John Soane, architect of the first Bank of England. He was appointed professor of architecture at the Royal Academy and made a collection of illustrations to use in his teaching. His art collection grew and he purchased a house in Lincoln's Inn Fields to accommodate it. Today his home is the Soane Museum, housing one of the most illustrious art collections in the world.

Whitchurch has a twin, Pangbourne, standing across the river at the confluence of the Rivers Pang and Thames. This town was granted its charter in the 9th century, but wears its years lightly. Kenneth Grahame, author of *The Wind in the Willows*, died here in 1932. His famous book had been written years before at Cookham Dean, originally as a series of letters to his only son, who was tragically killed when he was only 20.

ROUTE DIRECTIONS

1. Turn right on to the B471 towards Whitchurch and bear right again to go down the village street past the Greyhound and Ferryboat pubs.

2. Carry on and cross the toll bridge over the Thames (pedestrians go free) with the lock on your right, to arrive in Pangbourne. Turn left through the gates back on to the towpath.

1. Follow the towpath through Pangbourne Meadow and round the meander, passing, on the opposite bank, Hardwick House.

N

The house and church at Mapledurham, together with the restored mill, are a delight

PANGBOURNE MEADOW is now owned by the National Trust. It covers seven acres (2.8ha) and is another example of open, traditionally managed meadowland.

Hardwick House is basically a Tudor construction, with stone mullioned windows, steeply pitched roofs and great chimneys in warm red brick, but parts of it make it one of the oldest houses in England. The land hereabouts was in the possession of the de Herdewykes soon after the Norman Conquest, and it passed to the Lybbes family in the 16th century. The house was visited by monarchs, including Elizabeth I and Charles I. The latter played many a game of bowls on the great lawn which slopes down to the river. During the Civil War the house was badly damaged and had to be extensively repaired. In the 18th century it became the home of Mrs Lybbe Powys, whose published diaries make delightful reading.

Mapledurham is a very small village in a wonderful Thames-side setting. Alas, it is on the far side of the river from the Thames towpath and there is no right of way across the lock to reach it.

Mapledurham House, like Hardwick House, is a Tudor mansion. It was begun in 1585 by Sir Richard Blount. The Blount family were staunch Roman Catholics and they remained true to their faith through all vicissitudes, so it is not surprising that there is a priest's hole in the house and a secret passage leading to the church. St Margaret's is Anglican, but contains a Roman Catholic chapel where the Blounts were interred. Alexander Pope, the poet, himself a convinced Catholic, came here to visit the Blount sisters, Teresa and Martha. Mapledurham Mill is so remarkably beautiful that it has been called '...a perfect Constable subject'. It is the oldest working flour and grist mill on the Thames and has been fitted with a new undershot wheel so that it is in full working order. It is open to the public and the flour ground between the huge old millstones is on sale. Prior to renovation the mill had been converted to turn a dynamo to produce electricity for Mapledurham House and to pump water to the estate reservoirs.

ROUTE DIRECTIONS

1. Arrive at Mapledurham Lock.
2. Go through the gate, past the lock and out of the gates at the other end of the lock (it's not possible to cross the river here). Follow the path to another gate followed by a squeeze-stile. Turn right away from the river up Mapledurham Drive with housing on your left.
3. Turn left and then immediately right on to the road and cross the railway line. Turn left along Hazel Road and right into Skerrett Way.
4. Follow Skerrett Way and then turn right up the steps on the right to the main road. Turn left to the Roebuck Hotel.
5. Turn left at the Roebuck to take the footbridge over the railway and go down the steps to the Roebuck landing stage on the Thames. Turn right along the towpath with the railway embankment on your right and the Thames on your left.

Mapledurham with the weir opposite

MAPLEDURHAM LOCK was the first lock on the Thames to be mechanised. The earliest weir here was probably constructed during the 13th century to provide a head of water for the mill, rather than for navigation. It is mentioned during the reign of Edward I (1272-1307) in connection with a trial at the King's Bench. A poundlock was opened in 1777, and is in the parish of Purley; the weir is in Mapledurham, the boundary going along the middle of the river. Originally the new poundlock was to be called Purley Lock, but '...local custom proved too strong ...the old weir had been 'Mapledurham Lock' and the same title would stand for the new engine in the eyes of the bargemen'.

The Thames Path diversion away from the river through the Purley Park estate to the Roebuck is no new route alignment. In 1777, following the opening of Mapledurham Lock, a Mr Worlidge refused to sell land in Purley meadow for a towpath. He was threatened with compulsory purchase by the Thames Commissioners, but even this failed to shake him. The complaint went up in 1780: 'Inconvenient it is to take off the horses at Mr Worlidge's field, and go thro' a lane round his house. It occasions a delay of half-an-hour besides the additional labour'. Mr Worlidge fell ill at this juncture and was unable to continue the debate. In 1784 the Commissioners established a double ferry, one boat at the Roebuck landing stage and the other about a third of a mile upstream with that third of a mile of towpath on the opposite bank. Neither of these ferries now exist and the Thames Path right of way has still to skirt round what was once Mr Worlidge's field!

THIS APPROACH TO Reading from the west is remarkably pleasant, for the railway swings away from the river just below Appletree Eyot and a wide expanse of open land, allotments, meadow and public gardens are interposed between it and the towpath. This imparts a country atmosphere that belies the nearness of Berkshire's county town.

Reading is chiefly known as a large industrial and commercial centre. In fact, it is ancient, and the earliest known human occupation of the Reading area took place during the Stone Age. Later, there was an Iron Age occupation here, which gave way, in turn, to a Roman town, probably the river port for *Calleva Atrebatum* (Silchester), and then a Saxon settlement. The Saxons christened Reading, although in Domesday it is 'Reddinges'. The Saxon town, modern Reading's ancestor, was built on the River Kennet, not on the Thames, very sensibly eschewing the flood-prone Thames-side watermeadows. This explains why modern Reading has such a rural Thames frontage.

During the Middle Ages Reading was important. Henry I founded a huge abbey here,
an abbey which has now disappeared except for a few walls and a much altered gatehouse. Yet, as Hilaire Belloc wrote, Reading Abbey finds its nearest counterpart in Durham Cathedral. Were a traveller from the Middle Ages to come with us down the Thames today the feature whose absence would most apall him would be the great abbey – for although lying in a flat meadow and not perched on a towering river cliff, Reading Abbey possessed the same massive architecture and commanding presence that we can see at Durham.

King Stephen built a castle at Reading but this has utterly vanished. Perhaps Castle Street gives an indication of its whereabouts.

Caversham, Reading's smart suburb across the river, sprawls up the hillside away from the Thames. The church, St Peter's, shelters among trees looking down on the Thames. Originally Norman, it was rebuilt in 1878. However, the Norman doorway has been retained and inside is a Saxon font of Purbeck marble. Nutley Abbey was at Caversham.

②

Caversham Bridge, built in 1926

ROUTE DIRECTIONS

1. Carry on along the towpath past a small picnic site, with views to the Chiltern Hills across the river, and pass in front of Reading Marine Services Boatyard.

2. Keep on into the open meadows, still on the towpath which becomes an enclosed path and then a riverside promenade (owned by Reading Borough). Pass the Reading Rowing Club boathouse, the drinking fountain and the Three Men in a Boat pub.

Reading to Henley-on-Thames

9¼ miles (14.75km)

This section of the walk passes along the attractive riverfront at Reading and continues along the towpath through picturesque Sonning to Shiplake, where it leaves the river briefly. It returns to the towpath to reach Henley-on-Thames, site of the world famous regatta.

READING, AS AN industrial centre, has a noble pedigree. From the Middle Ages onward it flourished, like Abingdon, as a centre of the cloth industry and during the 19th century it developed as a corn-milling centre with grain brought down the

Kennet and Avon Canal.

The parish church of St Lawrence, near the market place, originally stood just outside the abbey gates, with the outer gatehouse actually attached to it. The poor fragments of the abbey itself lie in nearby Forbury Park. They include the gatehouse which was used as a school in the 18th century (Jane Austen was a pupil), and is now a museum. Massive Reading Gaol's most famous inmate was Oscar Wilde. He wrote *De Profundis* while imprisoned there in 1897.

Reading Museum and Art Gallery has excellent displays of local archaeology,

including Roman Silchester, and of the archaeology of the Thames. There is also a Museum of English Rural Life in the town, which belongs to Reading University.

ROUTE DIRECTIONS

1. Follow the tunnel under the approach to Caversham Bridge and continue past the National Rivers Authority's working wharf to Reading Bridge.
2. Beyond Reading Bridge continue past Caversham Lock and enter King's Meadow. Keep on the towpath with the playing fields and then the Tesco superstore to your right.

ROUTE DIRECTIONS

1. Cross over the mouth of the River Kennet by Horseshoe Bridge (the long slatted slopes were designed for draught horses, not walkers) and continue along the towpath past the gasometers.
2. Continue, passing the Thames-Kennet Marina on the opposite bank, and enter the Thames Valley Country Park.
3. Carry on through the nature reserve with the new office development on your right. Continue along the towpath as the river becomes more enclosed.

King's Meadow, between the railway line and the river

THE RIVER KENNET flows into the Thames under the railway bridge to which the horseshoe bridge is attached. This was built to carry the draught horses over the mouth of the Kennet. The horses would get up speed on approaching the bridge, be unhitched from their barge and cross the horseshoe bridge while the barge, powered by extra speed, drifted unaided across the river mouth, to meet the horses the other side. This had to be done with care, as the Kennet was no quiet backwater, but an important waterway. Navigable to Newbury, it is joined to Bristol by the Kennet and Avon Canal. This canal, originally engineered by John Rennie and opened in 1810, is well-known for its 106 locks, including the famous flight of 29 locks at Devizes. It was closed in 1950, due to dereliction, but has been reopened due to the efforts of the Kennet and Avon Canal Trust.

Thames Valley Country Park occupies part of an area that was formerly rough meadow. Part of the meadow has been put aside as a nature reserve and here, among the meadow flowers, John de Fornsete, a monk from Reading Abbey, wrote a little song in praise of the springtime of the year which has become one of the best-known of English part songs:

Sumer is icumen in - Lhude sing! cuccu. Groweth sed and bloweth med And springeth the wude nu -Sing! cuccu.

This is the dialect of Wessex, such as was spoken by Berkshire folk at that time, and the music that accompanies it allows it to be sung as a round by six people, four on the melody and two providing a ground-bass. It is the earliest known piece of harmonised secular music and must have been sung in Reading Abbey.

Reading Abbey was the grandest of the Cluniac houses, covering some six acres (2.4ha). It was founded by Henry I in 1121, who died in 1135 and was buried there. His funeral cortège came up the Thames (the first recorded instance of the river figuring in an impressive non-military pageant), with the riverside wharves of London draped in black, a black and purple canopy over the bier with candles lit for the repose of the king's soul, and solemn laments and chants played and sung by the monks from Reading. Even the weather took a hand in the mourning: it rained continuously.

SONNING REACH, with gentle slopes coming down to the Thames, is justly famed for its landscape, and lovely indeed is the approach from Reading along the Thames Parade beneath the wooded grounds of Holme Park, now the Reading Bluecoat School.

Sonning Lock is famous for its floral display throughout the summer and has frequently won the Thames Conservancy Best Garden Competition. Its most famous lock-keeper was James Sadler, who came here in 1845, and found time to write rustic verses. He was also a well-known apiarist and invented the Berkshire hive. This being so, it is hardly surprising that he wrote poetry on two particular subjects: the Thames and bees.

There has been a mill at Sonning Eye, on the Oxfordshire side of the river, since the 14th century. The present building dates from 1797, and was built by the Misses Rich. Today it has been converted into a 200-seat theatre with a restaurant in which patrons can enjoy a pre-show meal overlooking the Thames.

Sonning Bridge is a fine 18th-century brick affair with a causeway which carries the road over two islands. The bridge was saved from destruction by William Holman Hunt, the artist, and Sir Edwin Lutyens.

Sonning is a picture-book village, a beauty spot by anyone's reckoning, with stately brick Georgian houses and quaint cottages. During the 10th and 11th centuries it assumed great ecclesiastical importance as the centre of the diocese of Berkshire and Wiltshire. Later Sherborne (in Dorset), to which Sonning had been united, became the centre of the united bishoprics. But the attractions of Sonning were many and at the time of the Reformation the Bishop of Salisbury was still living at Sonning. Now nothing of the Bishop's Palace remains, except a mound in the grounds of Holme Park.

The old Deanery has vanished too, only part of its wall remaining. Behind this wall, which he took as his starting point, the architect Sir Edwin Lutyens built a new house in 1901 for Edward Hudson, owner of the magazine *Country Life*. The house, in Thames Street, is called Deanery Gardens, and its grounds were laid out by Lutyens' frequent collaborator, the inimitable Gertrude Jekyll.

ROUTE DIRECTIONS

1. Continue along the towpath, now known as Thames Parade, to reach Sonning Lock. Follow the lane to the bridge.

2. Turn left over the red-brick bridge and then right over the footbridge across the millstream to rejoin the towpath, with the Thames now on your right.

The approach to the lock at Sonning

LOWER
SHIPLAKE

A4155

SHIPLAKE

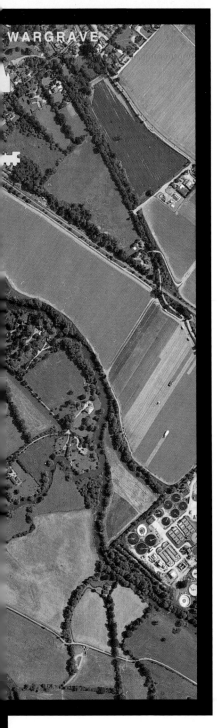

WARGRAVE

THE RIVER REACH from Sonning to Shiplake is a joy to walk, with meadows, woodland and parkland succeeding one another. On the stretch of river, beneath Shiplake College, the first Thames *Son et Lumière* was held in 1979. On the far side of the Thames the River Loddon flows in, its waters augmented by little St Patrick's Stream.

Shiplake Lock has a long history. There was probably a mill and weir here before Domesday. In 1404 the flashlock belonged to Elizabeth, Prioress of Goring. By 1585 it was generally known as Cottrell's (the name of the lock-keeper), and belonged to the crown. The poundlock opened in 1773.

In 1790 'Cotterell's Mill and Lock' was described as 'a very picturesque scene, highly deserving observation'. At this time there were two mills here, one for corn and one for paper, but by 1907 both had fallen into decay and were demolished.

ROUTE DIRECTIONS

1. Follow the towpath through the meadows on your left round several small meanders and through a small stretch of woodland opposite Hallsmead Ait. Shiplake College, formerly Shiplake Court, built in 1905 for Lord Phillimore, is visible on the slope to your left.
2. Cross the gated footbridge and continue along the towpath beneath Shiplake College to Shiplake Lock.
3. Cross the stile and turn left away from the river to a track. Turn right here and then left over a stile opposite Mill House.
4. Follow the path along the edge of the paddock and go over another stile. Keep the field boundary on your left and go up the field to turn left over the stile by the trees.
5. Cross the stile and go over the corner of the field to cross yet another stile into the driveway of Andrew Duncan House (this field is on the line of a former millstream and the old brick culvert is distinctly visible).

Shiplake from the south side of the river. Tennyson married his Emily here

LOWER
SHIPLAKE

A4155

① ② ③ ④

Looking beyond Shiplake to Wargrave on the other side of the river

LOWER SHIPLAKE, which is a recent settlement, clusters round the station. George Orwell lived at Roselawn in Station Road when he was a boy. Shiplake itself, with its Church of St Peter and St Paul, stands high on the wooded cliff over the river. The church is enriched by glorious windows of 15th-century French stained-glass which was saved from the sack of the Abbey Church of St Bertin at St Omer during the French Revolution and acquired by an enterprising vicar of Shiplake in the 1820s.

Here in June 1850 Tennyson married his beloved Emily after 14 years of courtship. As they drove away at the start of a blissfully happy marriage, Tennyson wrote a jingle to the vicar who had married them, hoping that the vicar's life might flow 'Smooth as Thames below your gates ...'.

Wargrave, across the river from Shiplake, is a lovely village and for years was the home of Gertrude Jekyll.

WARGRAVE

N

ROUTE DIRECTIONS

1. Turn left along the driveway and then right along Mill Road past the Lashbrook Cottages.
2. Bear right at the crossroads by the Baskerville Arms on to a road down to Shiplake Motors. Take the path on the right of the workshop and cross over the Henley branch railway line. Turn left along the path and then right into the gravel drive and left on to the road.
3. Keep on where another road joins from the left and continue on to the fenced path on the left of the private drive of Bolney Court.
4. Follow the path and cross over a track. Continue and cross the footbridge to regain the river bank.

A 423(T)

A 423(T)

P

P

HENLEY-ON-
THAMES

A 4155

③

④

②

①

Henley-on-Thames to Cookham

13 miles (20.75km)

Between Henley-on-Thames and Cookham the Thames Path passes through scenery in which everything seems to be on a larger scale than before. First, the long regatta course, then the tumbling weirs of Hambleden, the great meander bend and, beyond Marlow, the ascent up through Quarry Wood on to Winter Hill for a gloriously expansive view over the Thames valley before dropping back down again to reach Cookham.

MARSH LOCK is backed by a wooded hillside which adds an extra charm to the waters of the weir superbly viewed from the wooden causeway. There was a flashlock here in the 1500s and the poundlock was first constructed in 1773.

Henley is famous for its regatta which dates from 1839, a time when Henley was on the important coaching route from London to Oxford. Many distinguished guests stayed in the inns, including the Duke of Marlborough, who had his own room at the Red Lion. Travellers by coach would cross the splendid bridge which replaced an earlier timber structure that had been washed away by the river in March 1774. The 16th-century church stands near the bridge, its tall battlemented tower looking down on the scene. Charles Dickens described Henley as 'the Mecca of the rowing man', and it was the straight river reach between Henley and Temple Island that first attracted the rowing men to Henley. The races were first organised as a regatta in 1839 and the event became royal in 1851, under the patronage of Prince Albert. Today the regatta attracts rowing crews from all over the world who compete for the various cups and prizes.

ROUTE DIRECTIONS

1. Turn left along the towpath towards Marsh Lock. On reaching the lock bear right to follow the causeway to Marsh Lock Island and return to the river bank at Mill Lane along another long wooden causeway.
2. Turn right to continue along the towpath which joins a promenade as you approach Henley Bridge.
3. Where the promenade ends join the road and follow it past the Angel on the Bridge pub. Turn right to cross Henley Bridge.
4. Turn left on the other side of Henley Bridge and bear round to the left back on to the towpath with the river on your left (NB during Regatta Week in early July the path is moved inland, a fact recognised in the dedication of the right of way).

Most famous of all Thames-side towns – Henley

TEMPLE ISLAND, named after the mock temple built upon it in 1771 as an eye-catcher for Fawley Court, is the traditional starting point for races in the Henley Royal Regatta. The Mackenzie family owned it for over 130 years and sold it in 1988. Fawley Court, the red-brick house on the opposite bank, was designed by Sir Christopher Wren to replace an older house in which, on separate occasions during the Civil War, both Cavaliers and Roundheads stayed.

There was a mill and thus probably a weir at Hambleden in 1086. The present weatherboarded mill was built in the 16th century and has been converted into flats; but with the mill

REMENHAM

Wren designed Fawley Court and Capability Brown landscaped the parkland

house and tumbling weir waters alongside still makes up part of a delightful river-side group. The poundlock was built in 1773.

Caleb Gould was lock keeper here from 1777 to 1822. He lived to the ripe old age of 92, and is buried in Remenham churchyard beside his wife, Sarah, who had died long before him. W. H. Smith's great mansion, Greenlands, which gleams white across the river, is now a staff college.

Aston consists of half a handful of cottages and an inn near the site of a former ferry crossing. There was a rope ferry here in 1785.

ROUTE DIRECTIONS

1. Continue along the towpath past the hamlet of Remenham and past Temple Island (this stretch of river is the Henley Regatta course).
2. Follow the towpath round a wide meander bend past Temple Island to Hambleden Lock (with enormous weirs) and carry on past the lock (do not cross the river).
3. Turn right away from the river at Ferry Lane (site of Aston Ferry where the towpath crossed to the other bank) and go up the lane to Aston and past the Flowerpot Hotel.
4. Turn left along the private road to Culham Court and Holme Farm. Go through the swing gate just to the right of the farm buildings to follow the footpath to Culham Court.

MEDMENHAM ABBEY has a perfectly respectful medieval pedigree, but has become synonymous with the orgies of the Hellfire Club.

The Abbey of St Mary, a cell of the Cistercian Abbey of Woburn, was consecrated in 1200. At the time of the Dissolution only the abbot and one monk remained and Medmenham passed to the Duffield family. In the middle of the 18th century Francis Duffield granted a lease to Sir Francis Dashwood, who later became Chancellor of the Exchequer and then

ROUTE DIRECTIONS

1. Go through the gate and cross the bottom of the terraced lawn of the mansion, Culham Court.

2. Follow the path across the meadow. Go through the gate by Doorn Landscapes and follow the track past the estate cottages. Continue along the track to turn left through a kissing-gate into a field beside the PYO car park.

3. Head half-right across the field and cross the footbridge and stiles. Turn right back alongside the river.

4. Follow this path with the river on your left across three meadows, crossing a footbridge and stile at each boundary.

5. Keep to the riverside path opposite Medmenham (for views across to the abbey) and follow the path round the meander to Frogmill Farm where the path is surfaced (there used to be a fish weir here – note the islands).

Postmaster-General. Here the notorious Hellfire Club, whose correct title was The Society of the Monks of St Francis, met to indulge in their sacrilegious and obscene 'nameless orgies'. Their motto was 'Fay ce que voudras' (do what thou wilt), and certainly they did just that if the anecdotes told of them are true. The club was rumoured to include men of high rank, including the Prince of Wales and several cabinet ministers.

During Dashwood's tenure of Medmenham there were several Gothick additions to the place, including a ruined tower and an arcade and cloister facing the river. These remain substantially as they were intended, but the indecent ceiling paintings, pornographic inscriptions and erotic statues have not survived. Indeed, they have passed so indelibly into folklore that they have made Medmenham famous.

The ferry no longer crosses the Thames at Medmenham, but it was long-lived and had an interesting history from the day when Charles II was ferried across here in 1678. It made history in 1899 when the Court of Appeal deemed it to be public, and a monument commemorates the event. Frogmill was Frogg's Mill, a mill on the river. It may have been associated with Medmenham Abbey. The name 'Poisson Duc' on the cottages is a corruption of a Norman-French phrase relating to a fish weir or duct. Presumably the abbey had its fish weir hereabouts.

ROUTE DIRECTIONS

1. Continue alongside the river past a caravan site and a big boathouse into Hurley.
2. Go through the gate and turn left up the steps and over the wooden bridge. Turn right past Hurley Lock and then left over the river again by the horsebridge.
3. Turn left alongside the river with a meadow on your right and keep on passing, on the opposite bank, the entrance to Harleyford Marina.
4. Turn left over Temple footbridge and then right to follow the towpath, passing Temple Lock.

HURLEY WAS THE location of another Thames-side Benedictine priory attached to Westminster Abbey. Little now remains save the old refectory which once served as a stable block, a 14th-century tithe barn that is now a private house and a medieval dovecote.

The Priory Church of St Mary, which still exists, was consecrated in 1086 by Osmund the Good, Bishop of Sarum. This Norman church has a long narrow nave, with decidedly Anglo-Saxon proportions. It was restored in 1852. The Olde Bell, which claims to be one of the oldest inns in England, was once the priory gatehouse.

Hurley Lock was mentioned in 1580 and the poundlock opened in 1773. A remarkable relic that pre-dates the poundlock is the weir winch, whereby barges were hauled up through the flashlock. This can be seen on the left bank of the river immediately upstream of the present weir. Temple is named from the preceptory of the Knights Tem-

plar at Bisham. Temple Mills is where the knights' corn was ground. Subsequently it was used for flour milling then as a brass foundry and then a paper mill before the present residential development took place.

Temple Lock is only a short distance downstream from Hurley Lock. It too became a poundlock in 1773. The present lock was built in 1890 alongside the old lock.

The new Temple footbridge was built especially for the Thames Path.

HURLEY

N

The Priory Church of St Mary in the old
part of Hurley

MARLOW IS AN attractive old market town which has grown considerably in the last 50 years. It has a spacious main street and several interesting old buildings, including Marlow Place, built in 1720 for John Wallop who made it available for George II, when Prince of Wales, thus explaining the leek motif on some of the pilasters.

Thomas Love Peacock wrote *Nightmare Abbey* at 47, High Street and Shelley and Mary Godwin joined him there in 1816 after their return from Italy. Shelley and Mary then lived at Albion House where Shelley wrote *The Revolt of Islam*, while Mary wrote *Frankenstein*. A century later T. S. Eliot came here and lived in West Street. There may have been a bridge at Marlow in early times, for it is mentioned in 1309. The present suspension bridge was built in 1831 by William Tierney Clarke; it is a scaled-down version of his bridge at Hammersmith. Tierney Clarke's masterpiece is the Budapest suspension bridge across the Danube. The famous inn, the Compleat Angler, lies across the river from the bridge.

ROUTE DIRECTIONS

1. Continue with the river on your right. Bisham Abbey, now the National Sports Centre, is on the opposite bank. Arrive at Marlow.

2. Turn left before the bridge to take the paved way in front of Tierney Court. Turn right up the steps to cross the road opposite the church. Turn right to follow the footpath (signed to Marlow Lock and Bourne End).

3. Follow the path (Seven Corner Alley) alongside the churchyard to the Two Brewers pub in St Peter Street.

4. Cross the road and follow the narrow walled alley opposite on the right of the pub which twists and turns to the road. Turn right along the road past Thamesfield Gardens. Bear left with the road past Marlow Mill.

5. Turn right down the path and across the green to the river. Go under the road bridge and climb the steps to the A404. Turn left over the Thames.

6. Keep on the road on the other side of the river and then turn left down the steps and go along Quarry Wood Road. Turn left at the foot of the wooded river bluff where the road turns right.

The elegant suspension bridge at Marlow

1. Follow the path up through the woods.
2. Keep on this path where it nears the road again and continue along a level section to Dial Close, emerging at the road to the left of a house called Rivendell.
3. Bear left into the small car park and continue along the road with magnificent view over the Thames valley and the National Trust open area of Winter Hill to your left. Continue past a road junction to a house called Chimneys and bear left

on to a gravel track which heads downhill (signed Cockmarsh NT).
4. At the bottom of the hill turn left. Cross a stile and pass a pond on your right. Go diagonally right across the broad meadow to the white Ferry Cottage opposite Spade Oak Farm.

QUARRY WOOD, WHICH clothes the slopes of Winter Hill, contains some magnificent beech trees. It is thought to be the original 'Wild Wood' in Kenneth Grahame's *The Wind in the Willows*, written when he lived just over the hill at Cookham Dean.

The magnificent view from the top of Winter Hill encompasses the Thames valley from Bisham round to beyond Bourne End and the panorama of the great winding river and the Chiltern

Hills is much favoured by artists.

Winter Hill is well known in geological circles for one of the gravel terraces which has helped unravel the history of the Thames during the Ice Ages. The Winter Hill terrace stands at a height of about 270ft (82m), the level at which the river and its valley stood at the time the terrace was formed. However, the terrace does not turn south at Bourne End with the present river, but carries on eastwards through Beaconsfield and the Vale of St

Albans into Essex. When, during one of the Ice Ages, this exit was blocked by glaciers the river was diverted to the south, cutting its present valley.

Spade Oak Ferry, which no longer runs, dates from 1822 when it was necessary to ferry gangs of men and horses across the river to rejoin the towpath on the far side. At that time Spade Oak was an important wharf.

Winter Hill, a well-known viewpoint east of Marlow

N

COCK MARSH, WHICH is in National Trust ownership, faces Bourne End across the Thames. It is a fine example of wet lowland marsh, a habitat increasingly at risk today. The ancient history of the area is evidenced by a group of burial mounds.

For millennia the waters of the Thames have been used for navigation and other purposes – fishing, turning mill wheels, water supply, waste disposal. These uses, almost by definition, must conflict and the river has been subject to times of conflict and chaos prior to the development of the present ordered management system.

The history of the management of the Thames as a waterway begins in 1065 when Edward the Confessor decreed that there were four royal rivers – the Thames, the Severn, the Trent and the Yorkshire Ouse – and that on these rivers navigation was of paramount importance: 'If mills, fisheries, or other works are constructed to (navigational) hindrance, let these works be destroyed...'.

It is doubtful if the millers, in partic- ular, cared much to obey the royal command, for the sentiment was repeated, by monarchs and by parliament, down the centuries. In 1197 Richard the Lionheart sold his rights over the Thames to raise money for the Crusades and control passed to the City of London; who guarded this right jealously. At Staines there is still a replica of their boundary stone, set up in 1285 and known, appropriately enough, as the London Stone.

In 1215, Richard's brother King John, in Chapter XXIII of the Magna Carta, ordered that: 'All weirs from henceforth shall be utterly put down, by Thames and Medway...'. Despite this, the weirs did not vanish, and it seems that even at that time some boat- men recognised that in shallow stretches of the river the greater depth of water behind the weirs could be of help to navigation. But these brushwood weirs were constructed both to provide a good head of water for a mill wheel, and as fish traps, and

BOURNE END

tion above Staines.

In 1857 the Thames Conservancy Act transferred the City of London's rights to the new Thames Conservancy, but the river upstream from Staines was still controlled by the Commissioners. In 1866, however, the brief of the Thames Conservancy was extended to cover the whole river downstream from Cricklade, including the London reaches, thereby abolishing the Commissioners.

This changed again in 1909 when the Port of London Authority, which had been set up the previous year, assumed control of the tidal reaches of the the Thames, thus leaving the Conservancy responsible for the river above Teddington.

In 1974 the Thames Conservancy was absorbed into the Thames Water Authority, one of ten authorities constituted in an Act of 1973 to cover England and Wales. The TWA was responsible not just for navigation, but for the whole water cycle in the Thames basin, 'from source to tap', including water supply, fisheries and sewage disposal.

Control passed to Thames Water, the privatised TWA, and in 1989 the National Rivers Authority (Thames Region) took over. Their headquarters are at King's Meadow in Reading. Below Teddington the river is still in the jurisdiction of the PLA.

millers were very good at diverting water from the main stream into their mill streams.

The first organisation devoted solely to some co-ordination of navigation was the Oxford-Burcot commission, set up by James I in 1605. This was organised to try to deal with the notorious rocky shallows upstream from Burcot. At that time merchandise going upstream had to be carried overland from Burcot to Oxford, a distance of 14 miles (22km).

In 1624 an Act was passed commanding the appointment of Commissioners to oversee the clearance of the river and the building of weirs and locks and a towpath. Thus the first poundlocks were built on the Thames at Iffley, Sandford and in the Swift Ditch. Thames Commissioners were first appointed in 1729 and this body of 600 (an enormous committee!) was responsible for the Thames naviga-

N

ROUTE DIRECTIONS

1. Bear right to follow the towpath along the river past bungalows (at the foot of their gardens) and the Moorings Inn.
2. Pass under Bourne End railway bridge and into the open National Trust meadows of Cockmarsh and back into fields.
3. Still keeping to the towpath follow the meander bend round to Cookham.

Cookham to Windsor

10 miles (16km)

From Cookham to Windsor the Thames Path passes through some of the loveliest scenery in the Thames valley – the wooded Cliveden Reach – and then heads away from the Chilterns on to open meadows and into the royal town of Windsor, dominated by its great castle. The walking is easy throughout.

COOKHAM IS A spacious village with a big green known as Cookham Moor and a wide high street on which are two well known hostelries, the King's Arms and the Bel and Dragon which dates from 1417.

The church, Holy Trinity, which sits in a meadow beside the Thames, is mentioned in Domesday, while Cookham Mill is mentioned in 1369.

The artist Stanley Spencer (1891-1959)

found his inspiration in the scenes around Cookham and the Stanley Spencer Gallery is in the King's Hall, where Spencer attended sunday school as a boy. He is buried in Cookham churchyard, alongside the path followed from the river.

At Cookham the Thames splits into numerous channels to round the great meander bend and swing southwards past Cliveden. Cookham Lock Cut was

excavated in 1829-30 along the course of an existing channel known as the Sashes Stream, and the original course of the river was left to fend for itself. This is now known as Hedsor Water and is unnavigable, with a functioning weir at its upper end and the remains of a weir across it at the lower end. The lock is not on the Thames Path, which follows the Lulle Brook, once a millstream. My Lady Ferry, whose broken landing stage stands by the Thames Path opposite the great bank of Cliveden Woods, was one of three ferries to operate at Cookham. This was an ancient Thames crossing-place, possibly going back into prehistory. Cliveden Woods, which tower 200ft (60m) above the river along the 2-mile (3km) reach from Cookham to Maidenhead are part of the Cliveden Estate. Cliveden was the seat of the Duke of Westminster and afterwards of Viscount Astor and his wife Nancy, the first woman to sit as an MP. The present house was built in 1851 and was the

scene of many 20th-century political scandals, notably the Profumo affair of 1963. It is now in the hands of the National Trust who let it as an hotel to Blakeney Hotels Ltd.

ROUTE DIRECTIONS

1. Turn right past the church and between white cottages to the road. Bear right to the Stanley Spencer Gallery.

2. From the Stanley Spencer Gallery in Cookham go up Sutton Road and turn left into Mill Lane.

3. Bear right on to the hedged path between gardens, cross the drive and go over a stile. Bear right along a path through woodland, soon with the drive to Formosa Place on your left.

4. Bear right with the path and continue to reach the Thames at the broken landing stage of the old My Lady Ferry. Turn right on to the towpath along Cliveden reach (opposite are the beech woods of the National Trust's Cliveden Estate. The house is on the terrace above).

THE REACHES OF the river around Maidenhead speak of the years between 1870 and 1914, when the Thames upstream of London was no longer a commercial waterway (freight had transferred to the railways), but the aristocratic, fashionable resort of the south. Here, more than anywhere else along the river, we rub shoulders with the Golden Age of the Thames.

At Taplow Court, opposite Maidenhead, lived Willy Grenfell, later Lord Desborough, punting champion, brilliant all-round athlete, and for decades Chairman of the Thames Conservancy. Here Lord Desborough and his wife, the charming Ettie, entertained high society and brought up their children. Julian and Billy both perished in France in World War 1, and Julian's poem, 'Into Battle' became one of the best known of that era. When his father was given a peerage in 1905 Julian wrote a verse commemorating the fact.

At Maidenhead's Boulter's Lock presided W. H. Turner, the doyen of Victorian lock keepers, a courteous, 'gentlemanly' ex-naval gunnery and cutlass instructor. Boulter's Lock is probably the most famous lock on the Thames. There is a good reason for this: it is one of the busiest. During the summer season today many hundreds of craft pass through the lock daily. During the Golden Age London visitors, on reaching Maidenhead, which was a fashionable river resort, had to pass through Boulter's to get into Cliveden Reach, and Boulter's

became known as a bustling, noisy exciting place of recreation. It was traditionally extremely busy on Ascot Sunday. Numerous photographs and paintings of the river have Boulter's as their subject, but probably the most famous is Gregory's 'Boulter's Lock, Sunday afternoon' painted in 1895, in which a whole conglomeration of punts, skiffs, rowing boats, steamers and canoes crowd the narrow lock entrance, while their occupants, dressed to the nines, show evident good humour. Mr Turner was obviously very much in control.

There has been a lock at Maidenhead since at least 1580, the poundlock being installed in 1770 (the earliest of a set of eight poundlocks built under the legislation of 1770), and was ready for traffic at Michaelmas 1772.

The Maidenhead Steam Navigation Company run a 19th-century steamer, *Belle*. She is available for private charter for up to 80 passengers. Built in 1894 by Tooley's of Hampton Wick, and sold to a firm in Worcester in 1896, she was in a sorry state by 1980 when she was acquired by Ted Harris of the Maidenhead Steam Navigation Company and restored to her original condition.

ROUTE DIRECTIONS

1. Follow the towpath round to Boulter's Lock on the outskirts of Maidenhead, passing through a conservancy gate to Ray Mead Road, a riverside promenade.

Boulter's Lock with the very popular Boulter's Inn to the right

MAIDENHEAD

①

②

Brunel's original bridge has been doubled in width to provide four tracks

N

TAPLOW

A4

MAIDENHEAD OWES its prosperity to the bridge built here in 1297 on the road from London to the West. The present Maidenhead Bridge is a graceful structure in Portland stone, built in 1772-7 to replace the medieval bridge. It was designed by Sir Robert Taylor, who later left £180,000 to Oxford University to build the Taylorian Institute for language teaching.

Beside the bridge stands Skindles Hotel, frequented by Society. It was started by a local boy called Skindle who set up his establishment solely to cater for the upper-class pleasure-seekers from London. Many an assignation was arranged at Skindle's and the name of the hotel appeared in many a divorce court, yet Skindle managed to turn all this to his own good account!

The spectacular low-arched railway bridge was built by Brunel in 1839 to carry the Great Western Railway. It has two segmental arches, each 123ft (37m) long, which have achieved immortality in Turner's famous painting *Rain, Steam and Speed*. The central pier of the bridge rises from an island where the Guards Boat Club used to have its headquarters. This was the most exclusive of the social boating clubs on the river during the Edwardian era.

ROUTE DIRECTIONS

1. Keep on the road and turn left over Maidenhead Bridge.
2. On the other side of the bridge turn right along a small road to get back to the towpath. Pass under the great Brunel railway bridge (under one of the main arches, called the 'sounding arch' because of the echo).

JUST BEFORE REACHING Bray
the river turns past a succession of
riverside villas, in a great meander
loop. In 1891 one of the most
spectacular of the 'Venetian fêtes' to be
held on the Thames was staged here.
The firework set pieces included a representation of the Battle of Trafalgar.

Bray is the village of the famous
vicar, who, to save his position (for
the living was a fat one), changed the
colour of his religion to suit the times.
His tale, as told in the ballad, informs
us that during the reign of 'good King
Charles' (Charles II): 'A furious High-
Church man I was, And so I gained
preferment...'.

With the arrival of James II, the
vicar veered to the church of Rome,
back to the church of England, and
finally: 'The illustrious House of
Hanover, The Protestant Succession,

To these I lustily will swear, Whilst
they can keep possession...'.

But who was the vicar? Apparently
the historical person lived not in the
reigns of Charles II, James II, William
III, Anne or George I, but came from
an earlier age of even greater religious
upheaval, namely the reigns of Henry
VIII, Edward VI, Mary I, and Elizabeth
I, making him twice a Roman Catholic
and twice a Protestant... This man's
name was Symon Symonds. So
insensible was he of everything that
bore the name of moral honesty, that
instead of being in the least affected by
it, his constant answer was, 'I will live
and die vicar of Bray'.

Maybe this is so, but in Bray church

there is a monument to another vicar, Francis Carswell, who, between 1667 and 1709, also performed several religious U-turns.

Bray's old centre clusters around the large 15th-century St Michael's Church. It still has very much the air of a village, despite much new development and the proximity of the M4 which crosses the Thames by a bridge built in 1961. At the bottom of Ferry Lane, where the ferry used to ply the Thames, stands Michel Roux's acclaimed Waterside Inn.

Bray Lock, on the site of a mill which pre-dates Domesday, is famous for its garden. The lock itself was not built until the 19th century, and in 1840 the present weir stream was in use as the navigation channel. Improvements were made and the entire lock was rebuilt in 1885. Between the lock and the M4 bridge the towpath runs along Amerden Bank. From about 1770 onwards this was a real problem, as the landowner consistently obstructed this stretch of towpath. At one time things were so bad that a horse ferry had to be employed.

ROUTE DIRECTIONS

1. Continue along the towpath, with the river on your right and fields on your left, to arrive at Bray Lock.
2. Follow the towpath under the M4 (there is a footbridge here if you wish to cross to Bray) and along Dorney Reach through a white gate and past some houses.
3. Continue along the towpath (opposite the entrance to Bray Marina, a path, the Barge Path, turns off to the left for Dorney church and the Tudor mansion).

N

② DORNEY REACH ③

THE PATH OPPOSITE Queen's Eyot leads up to Dorney, which, despite much 20th-century development (including lots of mock Tudor), is remarkably unspoilt. The great house, Dorney Court, and the Church of St James stand back from the river on the same bank as the Thames towpath. Dorney Manor is mentioned in Domesday, but the present house is early Tudor, built around 1500. The pinkish brick house has tall chimneys and many gables, while inside are the original fireplaces and a fine collection of furniture and paintings. John Rose, who was later to be royal gardener at St James's Park, was head gardener at Dorney during the reign of Charles II, and it was here that he grew the first pineapple produced in England. Dorney's pub is called the the Pineapple, to the frequent curiosity of visitors.

The church groups perfectly with the house, though now it is among young trees, planted to replace the great elms that used to guard it. The stone-and-flint walls date back to Norman times, though the windows are more recent. There is a Tudor tower in brick.

On the opposite side of the river are Bray Studios, where the occasional glimpse of a film set adds a somewhat unreal tinge to a walk along the towpath. The studios occupy what was originally Down Place, the meeting place of the Kit-Cat Club, ostensibly a literary club, devoted to encouraging good writing, but clandestinely involved in supporting the Hanoverian Succession. Members included Sir Robert Walpole, Addison, Steele and Congreve. The club, reputedly, took its name from the baker who supplied the club with meat pies, one Kit Catt.

The next large house on the other side of the Thames is Oakley Court, or Water Oakley. It is a piece of Victorian Gothic, built in the style of a Rhine castle in 1859 and now a hotel. The surrounding evergreens give it a somewhat spooky air. Where are the bats?

The weir and lock at Bray

ROUTE DIRECTIONS

1. Carry on along the towpath with Dorney's enormous Thames Meadow on your left.

A308

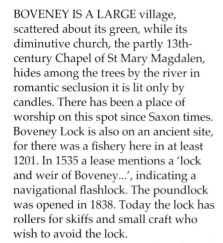

BOVENEY IS A LARGE village, scattered about its green, while its diminutive church, the partly 13th-century Chapel of St Mary Magdalen, hides among the trees by the river in romantic seclusion it is lit only by candles. There has been a place of worship on this spot since Saxon times. Boveney Lock is also on an ancient site, for there was a fishery here in at least 1201. In 1535 a lease mentions a 'lock and weir of Boveney...', indicating a navigational flashlock. The poundlock was opened in 1838. Today the lock has rollers for skiffs and small craft who wish to avoid the lock.

Windsor Racecourse, on the other side of the river, sits on what is technically an island, for it is enclosed by the Thames on one side and Clewer millstream on the other. Farther along the path comes 'Athens', marked by a little mound. In 1918 this was donated to Eton by Mr H. Baker of Bristol in memory of his son, killed in a flying accident in 1917.

Here, approaching the dominant bulk of Windsor, set high on its hill, it is hard to escape the illusion that the Thames is flowing not only through its own fertile valley, but through an even richer vale – the long centuries of history that it has seen.

Again and again the walker is reminded of the words of John Burns MP (1858-1943), the first working man to achieve cabinet rank. He was entertaining two Americans on the terrace of the House of Commons and, at length, irked by their tone, he gesticulated towards the river flowing past them, and said: 'Gentlemen, the Saint Lawrence is cold muddy water; the Mississippi is warm muddy water; but the Thames is liquid history'.

ROUTE DIRECTIONS

1. Continue to Boveney Lock.
2. Keep to the towpath past Boveney Lock and past 'Athens', the traditional bathing place for Eton College boys (look out for the concrete platform and tablet) before passing under the A332 road bridge and the railway bridge.

Eton College with the chapel on the right

141

Windsor to Chertsey

11 miles (18km)

This reach of the river begins with the great royal stronghold of Windsor, it passes by the very place where Magna Carta was signed and carries on past Staines, an ancient Thames crossing place. The path is easy, much of it metalled.

ROUTE DIRECTIONS

1. Follow the river bank with the open Brocas Meadow to your left and views to Windsor Castle ahead. Continue past Eton College boathouse and bear right past the Waterman's Arms in Brocas Street.

2. Turn right to cross the pedestrians-only bridge over the Thames to Windsor and turn left on to the quayside.

3. Go along the quayside and take Romney Walk, the path between railings just beyond the Donkey House pub. The railway is on your right with a brief glimpse of Eton College chapel across the river to your left. Bear right into the lane and follow it to a boatyard.

4. Bear left across the boatyard and cross the stile on to the towpath. With the river on your left, follow the meander round past Romney Lock, under Black Potts railway bridge and over playing fields.

5. On reaching Victoria Bridge climb up the bank and cross the white rail to turn left over the Thames (the towpath through Windsor Home Park is not open to the public).

6. Across the river bear right with the road (B470) and then turn left to follow the footpath parallel to the road along the edge of Datchet Golf Course.

7. Return to the road at Datchet.

④

⑤

A470

⑥

⑦

DATCHET

WINDSOR

WINDSOR CASTLE, the largest inhabited castle in the world, stands on a hill that is a natural stronghold. Both the early Britons and the Romans used it as such, for perched on its river cliff above the Thames the castle is visible for miles around and makes a forceful statement about the power of its royal inhabitants.

The building of Windsor Castle has spread over eight centuries, for it has been a royal residence continuously for 850 years, held in high regard by all our monarchs, though some seem to have been particularly attached to it. The present Queen, for example, uses Windsor far more than any of her immediate predecessors.

The castle consists of three basic parts, the Lower, Middle and Upper Wards. Entrance is on the Lower Ward, through the Henry VIII Gateway (so called, though it was built long before his time), and leads to the broad castle precincts, on one side of which is St George's Chapel, an outstanding architectural achievement. It was founded by Edward IV and dedicated to St George, patron of the Order of the Garter. Work started in 1478 but was not completed until 1511. Here, in

June, in a ceremony that has been taking place at Windsor for nigh on 650 years, the Queen invests new Knights of the Garter – their richly coloured heraldic banners hang in the choir – an order founded by Edward III.

The Middle Ward consists of Edward III's Round Tower, with its views over 12 counties, and North Terrace, which runs along the battlemented castle wall. From here there are fine views over the river to Eton, thought by some to be the view that Gray had in mind when he wrote his 'Ode on a Distant Prospect of Eton College'. The State Apartments comprise the Upper Ward. They are reached from the North Terrace and can be viewed when the Queen is not in residence. These magnificent rooms, richly furnished and hung with paintings by such great artists as Rubens, Reynolds, Holbein, Van Dyck, Durer, Memling and Canaletto, reach their apogee in the Throne Room and the Waterloo Chamber, which contains portraits by Lawrence of the men who played important roles in Napoleon's downfall.

On view too at the castle is Queen Mary's Doll's House, designed by Sir

Edwin Lutyens to the scale of 1in to 1ft (2.5cm to 0.3m). It is really a palace within a palace, containing a diminutive library (the books written especially by well known authors of the 1920s). The Royal Mews are outside the bounds of the castle proper, on St Albans Street. Here the royal horses, coaches and carriages can be seen.

The Home Park, to the east of the castle, crooked in the arm of the Thames as it swings past Datchet, is joined to Windsor Great Park by the 3 mile (4.8km) Long Walk. At the end of this is an equestrian statue of George III, generally known as the Copper Horse. The Home Park contains Frogmore House and the Royal Mausoleum at Frogmore, where Queen Victoria and Prince Albert are buried.

Windsor Great Park, the remains of a royal hunting forest, lies to the south of the castle and covers some 5,000 acres (204ha), a large amount of which is open to the public. The most important areas are the Valley Gardens, containing the largest rhododendron collection in the world, and the Savill Garden, which has rare plants from all across the globe.

The town that clusters at the foot of the castle is a bustling, ancient place, with narrow streets full of shops. Opposite Windsor Castle is the Royalty and Empire Exhibition, mounted by Madame Tussaud's Waxworks. Here, in wax, Queen Victoria is seen arriving to celebrate her Diamond Jubilee in 1897.

Eton, the small town across the bridge from Windsor, consists effectively of a long rambling high street. But the name has become synonymous with Eton College, the public school founded by Henry VI in 1440. It is apt that Windsor looks down on Eton, and that the Thames flows past it on its way from Oxford to London. It is not the oldest of the public schools, but was based on the model set by Winchester. The chapel, visible from the Thames path, is remarkably like that at King's, Cambridge. The Upper School was designed by Sir Christopher Wren.

Brocas Meadow, on the edge of Eton, appears to get its name from a wood near a castle. In Brocas Meadow the influence of the great school is keenly felt. The buildings are visible from behind the trees and the river reminds us of Eton's great rowing tradition, though it must be one of the youngest of the school's traditions for until the 1840s the river was out of bounds to the boys. Eton Bridge, now used only by pedestrians, is a lovely iron bridge of 1824. Below the lock, under the shadow of the railway bridge (built in 1850) is Black Potts, a famous fishing spot. Izaak Walton used to fish here by invitation of Sir Henry Wotton, Provost of Eton. Victoria Bridge and Albert Bridge were built in 1851, it is said to a design by Prince Albert. Albert Bridge was rebuilt in 1928. These two bridges were built to share the work originally done by a now-vanished Datchet Bridge which crossed the Thames from Windsor Home Park.

BETWEEN 1782 and 1785 Datchet was the home of William Herschel, who was appointed astronomer to George III after his discovery of Uranus. His telescopes adorned his garden. Datchet Mead is the place made famous in Shakespeare's *Merry Wives of Windsor* as the scene of the ducking of Sir John Falstaff.

Old Windsor Lock, with its long cut creating Ham Island, was opened in September 1822. The weir was constructed later, in 1836. From 1850, with increased competition from the railways, tolls here were suspended for a year at a time in a bid to win back the barge traffic. In the custom of the day the lock keeper was deprived of his wages. The weir has recently been rebuilt.

Old Windsor was once the seat of kings, though today it is a suburban spread. In the 9th century a village grew up here around the Saxon palace where Edward the Confessor held his court and even after the Norman Conquest Old Windsor was used as a royal residence. In 1110 associations with royalty ceased, for Henry I moved the court to Windsor Castle. Today, it is not known with certainty where the Saxon palace stood.

A short distance below Old Windsor

ROUTE DIRECTIONS

N

1. Follow the road round to Albert Bridge keeping to the left-hand pavement (the right-hand pavement is not complete).
2. Cross the Thames over Albert Bridge and turn left down the steps to follow the towpath, again with the river on your left.
3. Pass the weir and continue alongside the lock cut (it is impossible to follow the Thames itself around Ham Island) to reach Old Windsor Lock.
4. Continue along the towpath and cross the footbridge over a private dock. Continue and cross the footbridge over the marina entry and carry on along the gravel path. Cross a boatyard and walk along the terrace at Old Windsor.

Lock, where there are some seats beneath the trees, stands Old Windsor Priory, and next to it the 13th-century parish church, which was restored in 1863 by Sir G. G. Scott. The Bells of Ouzeley pub faces the river at Old Windsor. The original bells, from Ouzeley Abbey, are said to have been lost in the river here at the time of the Dissolution. Across the Thames is Wraysbury.

ATCHET

WRAYSBURY

④

A 328

N

ROUTE DIRECTIONS

1. Follow the path on to the road and pass Englefield Green. Continue between the two Lutyen's gatehouses and enter the open meadows of Runnymede (National Trust).

2. Bear left on to the footpath and follow it through Runnymede, bearing left through a swing-gate to return to the riverbank where the river swings away to the left.

WRAYSBURY

②

RUNNYMEDE HAS GONE down in history as the foundation of England's liberties and is visited by thousands each year, for, as every school child knows, King John signed the Magna Carta at Runnymede on 15 June 1215.

> Nursing wrath in his heart John bowed to necessity and called the barons to a conference on an island in the Thames, between Windsor and Staines, near a marshy meadow by the riverside, the meadow of Runnymede. The King encamped on one bank of the river, the barons covered the flat of Runnymede on the other. Their delegations met on the island between ... Today it is open parkland, backed by

the wooded slopes of Cooper's Hill. Lutyen's gatehouses lead to the area of memorials. The Magna Carta Memorial was presented by the American Bar Association to commemorate the 750th anniversary of the signing of the Magna Carta. The RAF memorial, built in 1953 to a design by Sir Edward Maufe, takes full advantage of its situation on the top of Cooper's Hill. The Kennedy memorial stands near by, on an acre of land given by the Queen to the American people.

BELL WEIR IS referenced towards the end of the 13th century. The poundlock was opened in 1817-18. Just beyond the lock the river flows under the M25. During the construction of the motorway bridge, which opened in 1978, Neolithic remains were found. There were also Bronze Age remains which suggest a riverside settlement here in the 8th and 9th centuries bc. The A30 bridge alongside was built in 1961.

The London Stone (city stone) stood for 600 years or so on the banks of the river, on the edge of Staines Lammas, to mark the upstream limit of the jurisdiction of the City of London prior to the establishment of the Thames Conservancy in 1857. A replica now marks the spot, the original being in Staines Library. It was the site of the ceremony of Claiming Jurisdiction. In this the Lord Mayor of London, with various dignitaries, walked around the stone, and after drinking 'God preserve the City of London' distributed money to the assembled crowd.

Staines today is a modern industrial and residential town in London's commuter belt which has expanded enormously over the last 30 years. Yet, the town is of ancient origin and has been an important river crossing since before the Romans. The Roman road from London to Silchester crossed here – mentioned in an Itinerary of Antoninus as a bridge, which was probably a ford reinforced with logs. Alongside this road the remains of a Roman settlement have been found. The first date from which we have any firm evidence of a bridge is 1228, when two oaks from Windsor Forest were granted by the Crown for its repair. Against the bridge on the left-hand bank of the river is the Riverside pub, occupying an historic site. An inn is thought to have existed here in Roman times and, like many Roman inns, is believed to have been called the Bush.

Staines was mentioned in documents of AD969 and again in Domesday. Yet there is little of ancient lineage to be seen in Staines. Some of the houses in the high street date back to the early 18th century. St Mary's Church has a tower said to be designed by Inigo Jones, while St Peter's, by the railway bridge, was built and endowed by an eminent Victorian Lawyer, Sir Edward Clarke.

ROUTE DIRECTIONS

1. Follow the towpath to Bell Weir Lock, go under the M25, pass a white city post and the London Stone on the far bank and arrive at Staines Bridge. Climb up the steps to the bridge and turn left.

The great leisure complex of Thorpe Park, with the emphasis on water amusements

STAINES

EGHAM
HYTHE

ROUTE DIRECTIONS

N

1. Across the bridge turn right past the Riverside pub into Clarence Street. Turn right through the car park and turn left on to the promenade. Cross the River Colne and walk through the riverside gardens.
2. Pass a large car park on your left and then turn left away from the river. Turn right opposite Staines Library and follow the road past the Thames Lodge Hotel. Continue under the railway bridge and bear right back on to the towpath.
3. Carry on along the towpath past Penton Hook and an exit channel for the Queen Mary Reservoir.

Staines, land of reservoirs, sprawling away towards the suburbs of London

PENTON HOOK LOCK CUT bypasses a long goose-neck of a weir stream, the original Thames channel, on which in times gone by Chertsey Abbey Mill was situated. This narrow neck of land was frequently flooded by water rushing down from Staines. In fact, by 1803 the narrowest part of the neck was only 50yds across and by 1809 Rennie had suggested it as the obvious place for a lock. The lock was built in 1815 but the weir was not built until 1846 and has subsequently been rebuilt. The river banks below Staines have been colonised by bungalows and other riverside dwellings; their gardens, bright with flowers, slope down to the river. The actress Ellen Terry (1848-1928) lived in one at Penton Hook.

Flooded gravel pits make up the extensive Penton Hook Marina, which covers some 80 acres (32.4ha), while Thorpe Park has been developed as a theme park with emphasis on water activities which include water gardens, thunder river, water bus trips and so on.

LALEHAM

①

M 3

CHERTSEY

ROUTE DIRECTIONS

1. Carry on along the towpath which gives way to a gravel walk. At Laleham join a road, Thames Side.
2. Continue along Thames Side under the M3 to Chertsey Lock. From here take the grass path between the road and the river to Chertsey Bridge.
3. Cross over Chertsey Bridge and turn left to follow the signed footpath between works buildings (W. Bates & Sons, boatbuilders; Electron Beam Processes etc). Beyond the industrial area bear left on to the gravel walk and cross the footbridge over the marina entrance.
4. Follow the path and cross the lane with houses on your left and bear right until you come to a junction of lanes. Bear right here (public footpath 9) and walk across the meadow to the far side.

Chertsey to Hampton Court

9 miles (14km)

Along this stretch of the Thames Path the pull of the great city begins to be felt, and from here houses crowd down towards the banks of the river. Alongside, however, are many open spaces and the path makes for easy walking. The Wey Navigation joins the Thames near Weybridge.

DR THOMAS ARNOLD, the famous Rugby headmaster, ran a small private school at Laleham from 1819 to 1828, and always regarded Laleham as his home. His son, Matthew Arnold, the poet, was born, lived and died here.

Laleham Park used to be the grounds of Laleham House, the ancestral home of the Earls of Lucan, a family associated with misfortune. In 1855 the 3rd Earl gave the order for the Light Brigade to attack at Balaclava, with disastrous results. The 7th Earl disappeared in 1974, when wanted by the police for questioning about a murder. There was a ford at Laleham at the point where the river flows away from the main road and later a ferry crossed at this point. Chertsey Lock was built in 1913. In 1955, during maintenance work, the weir collapsed sending the roaring waters of the Thames straight through the lock

Chertsey Bridge was built in 1780-82 by James Paine, but the piers settled and the settlement not only shifted the stone facing but caused bulging in the outer walls and the collapse of part of the parapet. This necessitated the rebuilding of the central arch and the use of tie-bars.

Chertsey possesses something of an 18th-century air, particularly around Windsor Street near the site of the vanished abbey. The church is large and airy, dating mostly from the 19th century, but the ancient custom of Ringing the Curfew survives here. It is rung daily between 29 September (Michaelmas) and 25 March (Lady Day) on the Abbey Bell, a 14th-century survival of the monastic house.

ROUTE DIRECTIONS

1. Turn left to follow the Bourne, with Woburn Park on your right across the stream, for a quarter of a mile. Turn right and cross the Bourne by the concrete bridge then turn left and then right, following the footpath sign to cross the meadow parallel to the electricity transmission lines. Go through the gap in the overgrown hedge.

2. Continue in the same direction with a hedge on your right. Bear right at the next field boundary and carry on with the hedge now on your left. Bear left at the caravan park.

3. Cross the stile and bear left across the meadow under the electricity transmission lines (note the spire of Weybridge church ahead). Cross the stile/gate and follow the path to the lane. Turn right along the lane.

4. Turn left along the path through trees after the first road hump. Cross the ditch by the footbridge and turn left along the towpath

beside the Wey Navigation (National Trust).

5. When you reach the Thames Lock turn right to cross the horse bridge over the Wey Navigation. Keep going along the footpath, past the small car park, to join the lane with a corrugated steel fence on your left. Turn right, cross the lane and go down the path to cross one of the Wey channels by a green-and-white footbridge to enter Weybridge.

6. Turn left down the path (Church Walk) past Church Walk Studios and continue in front of the cottages. Cross the road and continue along Church Walk to emerge at Thames Street beside the Old Crown.

7. Turn left down Thames Street and pass the moorings and the Lincoln Arms. Keep straight on through the rowing club car park where the road turns to the right.

8. Continue along the towpath with Weybridge Ait (D'Oyly Carte Island) in the river on your left till the river divides at the Desborough Cut.

9. Keep straight on along the towpath with the Desborough Cut on your left, passing under the two road bridges.

THE WEY NAVIGATION, which opened in 1670, was one of the earliest 'improved' rivers, for the great canal-building boom took place a century later. Originally, the Wey Navigation stretched up the River Wey only as far as Guildford, but in 1764 it was extended to Godalming. The stretch from the Thames to Guildford is now run by the National Trust. Until 1969 grain barges from London Docks came up the Thames and along the Wey Navigation to Coxes Lock Mill. After some experimental runs the trip was restarted, only this time from the Tilbury Grain Terminal, and using motor barges with a capacity of 65 tons each. Alas, Coxes Mill has shut down and the traffic ceased.

Weybridge takes its name from the River Wey which flows into the Thames here. In many respects it marks the frontier of suburbia, which stretches on towards the truly urban

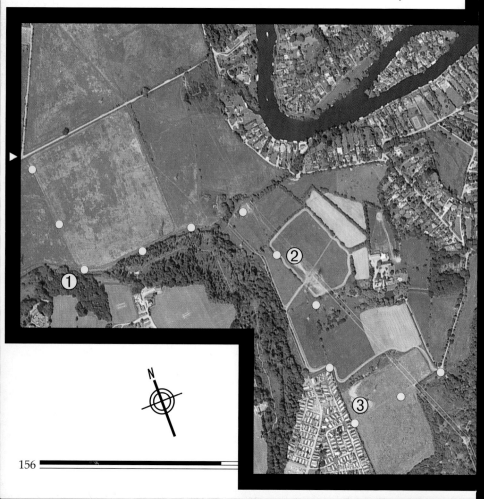

mass of London. This is an area where trees grow between the houses, where there are lawns, gardens and driveways. The ferry between Weybridge and Shepperton, which stopped running in 1960, is once again in operation.

In Weybridge is Oatlands Park, site of the Tudor palace built by Henry VIII for Anne of Cleves after he had divorced her. Some of the stones of Chertsey Abbey made their way into the walls of Oatlands, but they now have been dispersed even from here.

Shepperton Lock gets a mention as long ago as 1293. The present poundlock was opened in 1913. The weir stream is the most southerly point reached by the Thames.

WALTON-ON-THAMES has seen a great deal of new development, including a large shopping centre. The town hall was built in 1966, a piece of modern anti-architecture. In the church is a monument to Viscount Shannon, which, set up in 1755, dominates its setting.

Just upstream from Walton Bridge the Thames Path passes through Cowey Stakes, an open space of great interest. Local tradition maintains that this is where Julius Caesar forced a crossing over the Thames in 54BC, after he had given battle to Cassivellaunus. Tradition has, to some extent, been upheld here by archaeological finds which include British weapons of the period that were unearthed during work on the bridge approach in 1879. The name relates to some very ancient stakes found in the river here and mentioned by the Venerable Bede. These Cowey, Coway or Causeway Stakes marked the line of what had once been a ford. They were removed from the river over the centuries, as they formed a hazard to shipping, the last being taken up in the 19th century. In Book V of his *De Bello Gallico*, Caesar says:

> On learning the enemy's plan we moved up in full strength to the Thames, preparatory to entering Cassivellaunus's dominions. The river can be forded at only one point, and even there the crossing was difficult. Large native forces appeared in battle order on the far bank, which was also defended by a line of pointed stakes; and some deserters in our custody

revealed that more of these obstacles were planted underwater in the river-bed...

Obviously, the lines of stakes marking the ford have given rise to the tradition, though the place of Caesar's crossing could as easily have been at Staines or at Kingston upon Thames. Moreover, it has been suggested that the Thames did not flow in its present channel at Walton till the 10th century, and that the famous double row of stakes was probably either the piers of a bridge or the fence of a swimming way for cattle.

For some time now there has been a 'temporary' iron bridge in place at Walton, alongside the unsafe brick one. This bridge was painted by Turner and was the last in a series of bridges on this spot. It was built in 1864, the brick arches resting on the stone piers of an earlier bridge which was built in 1750 to an unusual design, for resting on the stone piers was a wooden latticework which gave the bridge a rather 'oriental' appearance. The idea, which proved none too easy in practice, was that unsound timbers could be replaced easily. It forms the subject of a painting by Canaletto.

ROUTE DIRECTIONS

1. Go under Walton Bridge and continue along the towpath, crossing the entry to a marina by a girder bridge. Carry on past the Anglers pub and the sports ground.

There is a confusing network of waterways at the junction of the Wey Navigation and the Thames at Shepperton

LOWER
HALLIFORD

WALTON
ON THAMES

①

SUNBURY HAS TWO locks, Old Lock, which was opened in 1886, and the larger New Lock, which was opened in 1927. There is a very wide weir stream and pool. The site of the original lock is marked by a footbridge and the old lock house, built in 1812.

Sunbury lies on the other side of the river and there is no right of way across to it. The Thames Path goes alongside the lock cut, and the lock island, on which are the moorings of the Middle Thames Yacht Club, is interposed between the path and Sunbury. Nonetheless there is a good view of it from beyond the locks. Sunbury still possesses that 'village feeling', despite its amazing Byzantine-style church, which was built in 1752 and reconstructed in 1856. Sunbury Court was built in 1770 and may have had some connection with Hampton Court. Originally known as Sunbury Place, it is now a Salvation Army Centre.

Swan upping, a tradition that goes back 800 years, starts in the third week of July at Sunbury. During the Middle Ages swans became much prized as food, and were regarded as royal birds, so much so that the Crown claimed ownership of all swans found on common water. Today, most of the swans on the Thames belong to the Crown, but the rest belong to two City of London Livery Companies, the Dyers and the Vintners. These companies are the direct descendants of the Craft Guilds of the Middle Ages, and they acquired their swan rights in the 15th century.

The purpose of swan upping is to mark the year's cygnets to establish ownership. Swan markers in double sculling skiffs, wearing a colourful costume, trail up the river in style, catching the cygnets to mark their beaks. The birds are given one or two nicks on their beak according to whether they are claimed by the Dyers or the Vintners. Royal swans have been exempt from marking since 1910. Presiding over this colourful ceremony (from his ceremonial skiff), dressed in scarlet livery, is the Queen's Swan Keeper, Mr John Turk of Cookham.

ROUTE DIRECTIONS

1. Continue to the Weir Hotel, where the path widens into a surfaced road, and continue on to Sunbury Locks. Keep going along the towpath with two reservoirs on your right.

Sunbury Lock. The village cannot be reached from the Thames Path

MOLESEY LOCK WAS rebuilt in 1906 (the largest lock on the river with the exception of Teddington: 265ft (80m) long and 25ft (7.5m) wide. The weir, which was painted by Sisley from the far bank, is not visible from the Thames Path.

Hampton, on the far side of the river, is still linked to the right-hand bank and the Thames Path by a ferry. The village itself still retains its late 18th-century charm, though the river is dominated by St Mary's Church, built by Lapidge in 1831 following the demolition of the earlier church. The village is close to Hampton Court, but takes its name from Hampton House (now Garrick House), bought by David Garrick, the great actor, in 1754. He converted it into a sumptuous residence and had the façade altered by the Adam brothers.

Chippendale designed the furniture and 'Capability' Brown, a friend of Garrick's, laid out the gardens. The house and gardens were bisected by the new turnpike road, but Brown overcame this difficulty by tunnelling under the road. Garrick's Temple, which stands by the river, was built to house Roubiliac's bust of Shakespeare.

In Garrick's time Hampton House became a centre of fashionable society, with all the names of the day stopping over to dine. Garrick was a superb host and, as the 'Gentleman's Magazine' observed, celebrated his silver wedding in 1774 by organising 'a splendid entertainment or Fête Champetre at his gardens at Hampton...' in which '...the Temple of Shakespeare, and the gardens, were illuminated with 6,000 lamps and a Forge of Vulcan made a splendid appearance'.

Above Molesey Lock are Ash Island, where T. W. Allen's boatyard has some Edwardian-style cruisers for hire, and Tagg's Island, named after Tom Tagg who once owned it. This has been a centre for traditional Thames houseboats since the days of Queen Victoria.

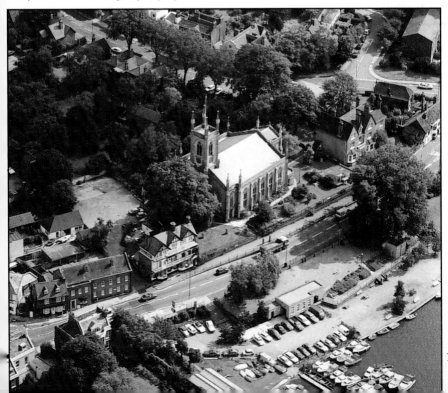

HAMPTON

ROUTE DIRECTIONS

1. Carry on along the towpath to Molesey Lock,
passing, on your right, the grassy old Hurst Park Racecourse.
Continue along the drive to the riverside road at the war memorial.

Hampton church stands right by the ferry which crosses to the other bank

Hampton Court to Richmond

8 miles (12.75km)

Although this last stretch of the route to Richmond is within Greater London, it is still a thoroughly enjoyable riverside walk throughout – and amazingly countrified. The Thames passes the great palace of Hampton Court and the magnificent Ham House, before reaching the tideway to become London River.

THE PRESENT Hampton Court Bridge was designed by Lutyens and built in 1933. It is the fourth bridge to cross the river at this spot and was designed so as to harmonise with Hampton Court Palace. Beside it is the Palace Boathouse, which hires out rowing boats.

The River Mole flows into the Thames just below Hampton Court Bridge, giving its name to Molesey, which is mentioned in Domesday.

ROUTE DIRECTIONS

1. Continue to Hampton Court Bridge and turn left across it.
2. Turn right to rejoin the towpath in Hampton Court Park with the great palace on your left.
3. Keep going along the towpath (Barge Walk) round the large meander with the river on your right. Along this reach the River Mole enters the Thames on the opposite bank. Arrive at Kingston Bridge and turn left across it.

KINGSTON
UPON
THAMES

THAMES
DITTON

HAMPTON COURT

HAMPTON COURT PALACE, generally acknowledged to be the most magnificent secular building in England, was originally built by Cardinal Wolsey. The son of an Ipswich butcher, his rise in both church and state was rapid. In the early years of Henry VIII's reign Wolsey was made

Lord Chancellor and was to become the most powerful man in England after the king, living in great pomp and splendour. The manor has been the property of the Knights Hospitallers for several hundred years when Wolsey acquired it. He began building the palace in 1514 but Henry VIII was angered at the unashamed showiness and magnificence of the palace and when Wolsey's position became precarious, Wolsey felt obliged to present it to his king. In return he was granted the manor at Richmond. Henry VIII immediately began to spend a vast sum to establish Hampton Court as a great royal palace. It was here that he courted Anne Boleyn and the initials HA are inscribed in a love-knot over the gateway.

The part of the palace erected by Wolsey and Henry VIII overlooks the river. This includes the Great Gate House and the Clock Court, which are part of Wolsey's original palace, and the Great Hall, 60ft (18m) high, 100ft (30m) long and 40ft (12m) wide, which was built by Henry VIII.

In later years Wren worked on the palace, building the East Front and South Front for William and Mary. This part of the palace contains private suites for distinguished visitors. During its years as a palace Hampton Court was the residence of 12 successive monarchs and several historic events took place here. The first was the courting of Anne Boleyn by Henry VIII, and in the reign of Elizabeth I the second trial of Mary, Queen of Scots, took place here. Later, under James I (Mary's son), Hampton Court was the meeting place for the famous conference that led to the King James Authorised Version of the Bible. James's son, Charles I, was kept here under house arrest in 1647 during the Civil War, and escaped by crossing the Thames in a wherry. The last monarch to inhabit the palace was George II, who died in 1760.

Today, part of Hampton Court is inhabited by Grace and Favour residents such as officers' widows and other pensioners, and by palace workers. The rest of the palace is open to the public.

The Formal Gardens are at their best in mid-May and include the Great Vine, which was planted in 1789, and the famous Maze (where Harris in *Three Men in a Boat* managed to get so hopelessly lost), which was planted for William III. There is the avenue on either side of the Long Water which was constructed for Charles II.

Bushey Park, famous for its deer, lies behind the palace. It covers 2,000 acres (810ha) and is laid out in a formal design reminiscent of Versailles.

HAMPTON
WICK

KINGSTON
UPON THAMES

KINGSTON BRIDGE WAS built by Lapidge in 1825-8. It replaced a wooden bridge which was the scene of the last recorded use of a ducking stool. 'Last week, a woman that keeps the 'King's Head' ale house, Kingston, in Surrey, was ordered by the court to be ducked for scolding, and was accordingly placed in the chair and ducked in the River Thames under Kingston Bridge, in the presence of two or three thousand people.'

The Royal Borough of Kingston upon Thames is an ancient and historic place. In AD836 Egbert, the first king of England, summoned his nobles and bishops to High Council here. Seven Saxon kings were crowned here, the last being Edward the Martyr in AD975, and their Coronation Stone is still to be seen outside the 1930s guildhall. Indeed, Kingston's old name, 'Kynggestone', is perpetuated on the town seal.

The town centres on the market place, but for all its historical importance Kingston has no real antiquities. Buildings of a number of periods are to be found. The parish church of All Saints is in the Perpendicular style, but the central tower was built in 1708. The town hall dates from 1838-40 and is built in the Italianate style. The guildhall and assize court date from 1934. On London Road is the mainly Tudor Lovekyn Chapel.

Kingston's lack of visible antiquities is counterbalanced by its archives. The town enjoys the rights conferred by 26 ancient charters, the first of which was granted by King John in 1199. Charles II granted a Wednesday market by Royal Charter, including the provision that no other market could be held within a 7-mile radius (11km); while in 1927

George V confirmed Kingston's title of Royal Borough. To the east is Coombe, where the author of *The Forsyte Saga,* John Galsworthy (1867-1933) lived. Hampton Wick is across the river from Kingston. Today it is marked by a timber yard. In 1914 Tom Sopwith's 'Schneider Trophy' seaplane was fitted with floats at Burgoine's yard in Hampton Wick, and the vehicle was tested on the Thames.

Teddington, across the river, was the home of the Irish comedy actress Peg Woffington (1714-1760) and of R. D. Blackmore (1825 -1900), author of *Lorna Doone.* His house, Gomer House, was demolished in 1939, but stood at the end of Doone Close, near the station.

ROUTE DIRECTIONS

1. On the other side of Kingston Bridge turn right down the ramp and then right again under the bridge on to the riverside walk.
2. Continue, with the river on your left, past the Bucklands Wharf development with the timber yard opposite. Bear right and then left on to the riverside road past Turks Launches (offering river trips on a variety of craft, including *Southern Belle,* a scaled-down version of a Mississippi paddle steamer) and boatbuilding yard. Continue under the railway bridge.
3. Carry on along the walkway beneath the plane trees with the river to your left, past derelict Kingston Power Station which is well hidden behind a row of poplars.
4. Take the road just beyond the Boaters Inn at Stevens Eyot and then take the riverside path to Teddington weir.

Hampton Wick on the left, Kingston on the right and central London straight ahead

TWICKENHAM

A 305

TEDDINGTON

HAM

②

①

N

THE THAMES IS TIDAL from Teddington downstream, and although there is a half-tide lock and movable weirs at Richmond, Teddington Lock forms the obvious dividing line between the non-tidal river of the pleasure boat and the tidal river, on whose lower reaches there is still a great deal of commercial shipping.

About 265yds downstream from Teddington Lock, on the right-hand bank and just off the towpath, is the stone obelisk marking the boundary of jurisdiction between the Port of London Authority and the National Rivers Authority, Thames Region.

The flow of the river at Teddington varies seasonally from an average of 400 million gallons daily in the summer to 15,000 million gallons daily during the winter. During times of drought the figure drops. In the 1976 drought it was down to 50 million gallons daily.

Teddington has the largest locking system on the river. There are three locks, of which the original is now known as the Old Lock. This was constructed in 1811 and rebuilt in stone in 1858, the same year as the tiny skiff lock was opened (known as the 'Coffin Lock' because it is so tiny). The enormous barge lock, built in 1904, is 650ft (197.5m) long, designed to accommodate a tug and six barges. The locks were all rebuilt in 1931.

Teddington's first weir was constructed in 1812; it was merely an overfall right across the river, with a central paddle-controlled rimer section. The weir was reconstructed in 1897 and the two roller sluices built in 1932.

Twickenham, across the river from the Thames Path, was a fashionable and elegant land of villas during the 18th century. Residents included such worthies as Jonathan Swift, Horace Walpole, Henry Fielding, Alexander Pope, William Chambers and John Gay. The area around St Mary's Church retains much of its 18th-century feel. The church possess a medieval Kentish ragstone tower though the main body of the church was rebuilt in 1714. Alexander Pope, the poet, and Sir Geoffrey Kneller, the portrait painter, are buried in there.

Dial House stands near to the church. This was presented to the church to be the vicarage by Thomas Twining, founder of the tea and coffee firm. It has a blue-and-gold painted sundial with the inscription 'Redeeming the Time'.

Alexander Pope had a famous villa at Twickenham, but the site has been developed by a Roman Catholic convent. The grotto, though it has lost its splendour, is still visible beside the road.

Ham House is a superb Jacobean mansion. Now in the hands of the National Trust, it is the historic home of the Tollemache family. It was built in 1610 and the exterior is mostly by Sir John Vavassour. Inside the plaster work is exceptionally good and the house contains an excellent collection of period furniture.

Eel Pie Island gets its name from the large number of these fish that could be caught hereabouts in the 18th century. In Edwardian days it was the resort of elegant tea dances, but by the 1920s there was a jazz club here and in the 1960s the hotel on the island had become home to a noisy nightclub featuring top rock groups. Eel Pie Island is one of the largest on the Thames – a world of bungalows on raised piers, of shacks, of the Twickenham Rowing Club, of boatbuilders and repair yards, and new housing on the site of the Victorian hotel.

ROUTE DIRECTIONS

1. Continue downstream to Teddington Lock (there are three locks here) where the Thames first feels the pulse of the sea. From Teddington downstream the river is tidal.
2. Continue along the towpath with Ham fields on your right and round the meander bend on to Ham Lands and the car park for Ham House (National Trust). A ferry from the landing stage here will take foot passengers across the river to Twickenham for 30p. Ham House is hidden behind trees to the right. To the left is Eel Pie Island.

ISLEWORTH

Symmetry at Kew Gardens: the Palm House

RICHMOND IS AN attractive riverside town which climbs up the side of Richmond Hill. It was fashionable in Georgian times, and the well-to-do flocked here to gain a brief respite from life in town. The centre is Richmond Green, an area surrounded by 18th-century houses and the theatre of 1899.

Today, Richmond Hill is crowned by the Star and Garter home for disabled servicemen which was established in 1925 and built on the site of the old Star and Garter Hotel.

Richmond Park covers 2,000 acres (810ha). It was closed originally by Charles I in 1637, and during the reign of George II there was an attempt to exclude the public. This resulted in a famous lawsuit of 1758, as a result of which the public have a right to free use of the park for all time.

ROUTE DIRECTIONS

1. Continue along the towpath, with Marble Hill (the white Palladian villa) on the hill over the river to the left, and on through Petersham Meadows.
2. On the approach to Richmond Bridge the towpath joins Richmond Terrace. Carry on along the Three Pigeons to Richmond Bridge.

THE TIDAL THAMES

JUST AS ABOVE OXFORD the Thames is known as the Isis, so below Teddington it is called London River, the tidal highway on which the great city was born. Below Teddington the Thames enters another world, a world which is at once commercial, international, urban and modern, whereas the non-tidal river above Teddington is recreational, English, rural and traditional.

Richmond Lock is the last lock on the Thames. Built in 1894 as a tidal lock, it improved the navigation between Richmond and Teddington. Downstream from Richmond, through Kew, Mortlake, Chiswick, Hammersmith and Barnes, the tideway flows serenly through west London. Then comes Putney, facing Fulham on the left, site of the Bishop of London's main residence, Fulham Palace. Elegant Putney Bridge was built in 1884 to replace an 18th-century wooden bridge that had become unsafe. This is the start-point of the Oxford and Cambridge boat race, a 4-mile (6.4km) course up the tide way to Mortlake, held annually in March or April.

Downstream from Putney Bridge the tidal Thames was formerly increasingly industrial. Today it is less so, though lingering pockets of industry remain. One of these, the Wandsworth riverfront, comes next along the right bank.

Wandsworth is home of the Young's Brewery, but until the 18th century was a village along the River Wandle, famed as a trout stream.

Beyond Wandsworth comes Battersea, where the old warehouses have been pulled down and development is in hand. On the opposite bank stands Fulham Power Station and Lots Road Power Station, the latter still providing electricity for London's underground network. The expensive new Chelsea Harbour development near by is nearing completetion.

Beyond Albert Bridge the Thames is confined between high embankments which deepen it and speed up its flow. Nonetheless you will still see youngsters fishing for roach, dace and eels, especially at low tide when wide swathes of mud, colonised by gulls, line the edges of the channel.

Here Chelsea Embankment faces Battersea Park on the south bank, and the fearful wreck of Battersea Power Station, half demolished and open to the elements. On the north bank the Tate Gallery and the Millbank Tower are followed by the noble spectacle of Westminster. Opposite, on the right bank, is Lambeth Palace, residence of the Archbishop of Canterbury since the 12th century, and County Hall, former seat of the Greater London Council that has now fallen on hard times.

Then comes the South Bank complex, its broad terraces looking across towards Victoria Embankment and Somerset House. Farther along is Bankside, overshadowed by the power station. In the 16th century this was Theatreland; the Globe, the Rose and the Swan were all here, as were inns and amusement gardens.

Southwark Cathedral, on the south bank, stands at one end of London Bridge, while Vintners' Hall, Fishmongers' Hall and the old Billingsgate fish market stand on the north. The Fishmongers' Company oversees the oldest annual sporting competition and longest rowing race in the world, the Doggetts Coat and Badge Race for Thames Watermen. It was started in 1715 by Thomas Doggett, an Irish comedian.

Until 1749 the only bridge over the Thames in London was London Bridge, which since 1176 had been a fantastic affair with houses and shops on it. The old London Bridge, with its 20 arches, restricted the flow of the river and allowed it to freeze – so giving rise to the Frost Fairs – until it was demolished in 1831.

Beyond London Bridge is the Pool of London, with the mighty Tower of London on the north bank. The Tower has seen use as a palace, a fortress and a dungeon since the White Tower was raised in 1078 by William the Conqueror. In former days the Pool was a forest of masts and a maze of shipping. In the 1790s new docks were authorised by Parliament under the auspices of the West India Company.

From Tower Bridge, London River swings round into Limehouse Reach, with the Isle of Dogs on the left. This is docklands, the area left derelict when the working docks closed in the 1960s, and now rising from the ashes in the new docklands development. Opposite the Isle of Dogs is Greenwich, famed for its royal and naval connections: the Queen's House, the Royal Naval College, the National Maritime Museum and, at Greenwich Pier, the famous teaclipper, the *Cutty Sark*.

Beyond Greenwich is the Blackwall Tunnel, and then Woolwich and the Thames Barrier. This flood barrier has been designed to prevent disastrous flooding in London, such as could happen were a surge tide to build up in the North Sea and be funnelled up the estuary. Movable barriers lie along the riverbed but can be raised to hold back the tide.

Beyond the barrier, the Thames is truly tidal as it flows under the new east London river crossing. Then the estuary widens out to the open sea, and the stream we have followed from its tiny beginnings is lost in the ocean.

Shepperton Lock

Index